HOW TO START A VENDING MACHINE BUSINESS

EARN FULL-TIME INCOME ON AUTOPILOT WITH A SUCCESSFUL VENDING MACHINE BUSINESS EVEN IF YOU GOT ZERO EXPERIENCE (A COMPLETE BEGINNER'S GUIDE)

WALTER GRANT

MATT COLEMAN

CONTENTS

INTRODUCTION

Dream big. Start small. But most of all, start.

SIMON SINEK

CAPITALIZING ON OPPORTUNITY

A few years ago, Ron was just a young, working-class man who aspired to start his own business. He wasn't your typical A-student in college, and didn't have a large network of friends to expose him to better work opportunities. But he knew one thing for certain—he was going to achieve financial security by the age of 32.

In his late twenties, he managed to land a position in a local computer company which handled the maintenance of vending machines. His job gave him the opportunity to understand the nitty-gritties of the business, which solidified his interest in it. He got to learn about the different types of vending machines, the best locations for vending machines, and all of the legal paperwork that is involved.

Once on an on-field task, he stumbled upon a local supplier of vending machine parts which revealed the general cost of parts and maintenance. Learning about the astonishing margin that companies charge on maintaining vending machines, Ron decided to start his own business where he provided maintenance services for vending machines.

His strong will, coupled with the sound knowledge of the intricacies of vending machines helped him chart a course to a successful vending machine business plan. After going through a series of hardships and denials, Ron finally found a venture capitalist who showed interest in his business and offered $50,000 in return for shares in his business. This solidified Ron's future and allowed him to achieve his dream of financial security before his 32nd birthday. Ron went on to build a successful business that drew him $300 per vending machine, per month.

VENDING MACHINES: YOUR TICKET TO FINANCIAL SECURITY?

Browse through social media and you will find a handful of business coaches selling programs to get you rich instantly. Of course, these programs only profit the creators and do little in sharing practical entrepreneurial skills. Many people—like Ron, who are tired of the unfulfilling 9-to-5 work life and desire financial security—fall victim to these schemes and never truly walk away with any real value.

This book is the perfect startup guide for building a successful vending machine business. For a fraction of what you would have paid for an online program, you will get insider advice and strategies on how to get your business up and running. The authors of this book have built seven-figure businesses based on the knowledge they are going to share with you in the upcoming chapters. What you are about to learn isn't textbook information, but real business lessons that can increase your likelihood of entrepreneurial success.

You might be wondering: Why vending machines? After all, the vending machine industry isn't the most glamorous out there. Okay, fair enough, the vending machine business isn't as cool as a tech startup, but that isn't what attracts most investors and entrepreneurs to it. Simply put, there is a lot of money to be made through operating vending machines.

The United States alone is home to a third of the 15 million vending machines around the world. Out of the 5 million vending machines located in the U.S. only 2 million are in operation. Nevertheless, in 2020, amidst the global pandemic, these 2 million vending machines brought in a total of $7.4 billion in annual revenue for their owners.

But big profits are not the only factor that makes this niche industry attractive. If you look at the vending machine market, you will notice that it is made up of a collection of small-to-medium sized businesses, scattered all across the country. According to research conducted by the *Hustle* magazine, there is no single vending machine company that owns more than 5% of market share (The Hustle, 2020).

It is true that conglomerates in the beverages industry own and operate a handful of vending machines, but the margins per machine are so slim that the vending machine model isn't suitable for large companies. This industry was created for the underdog, the aspiring small business owner, who can start out by owning a single machine and gradually scale their business while minimizing overhead.

You might have doubts about starting a business due to limited skills, funds, or knowledge about the world of entrepreneurship. However, starting a vending machine business is perhaps the most startup-friendly and doesn't require an exorbitant amount of money. This business model is a great way to bring in extra revenue every month and get hands-on experience running a business without investing too much of your time (or hiring too many staff). And if your first vending machine is a success, you can rinse and repeat the process in another location, and double your income!

The authors of this book, Matt Coleman and Walter Grant, are creative entrepreneurs with strong business acumen, and have built successful startup businesses. Both of them ended up leaving their corporate jobs to pursue entrepreneurship. The journey wasn't easy, and after a few business setbacks, they came across the vending machine business model. Being owners of two successful vending machine brands, the authors aim to help aspiring entrepreneurs start their new and profitable ventures and obtain the financial stability they have always dreamed of!

After reading this book, you will gain the confidence and know-how to start your own vending machine business from scratch. Yes, this includes information on how to register your business, and even tips on how to pick the right name. You will also get first-hand information on planning and designing your business so that it can operate with very little human effort. The solutions offered to you in this book are cost-effective and won't set you back financially.

Why wait another year to start your business when you have been given all of the tools? The future you have been dreaming about starts right now!

CHAPTER 1
STARTING A VENDING MACHINE BUSINESS: WHY BEFORE HOW

A SNAPSHOT OF THE INDUSTRY

About two years ago, during the peak of the global pandemic, the U.S. vending machine industry was valued at roughly $8 billion. You can imagine how much the high demand and low supply of goods put a lot of operators under severe pressure, yet the industry was able to perform better than most.

The industry's bounceback has been impressive. Market analysis shows that the industry is estimated to be valued at $8.9 billion in 2022 (IBISWorld, 2021). Although the vending machine market is relatively small compared to other retail markets (ranked 51st in the U.S. retail industry), it is nonetheless attractive to budding entrepreneurs.

What's more, entrepreneurs are given the opportunity to compete in various market segments within the industry. For example, if you think that selling beverages inside your machine is overrated, you can sell ready-made meals, cosmetics, or newspapers and magazines.

The same goes when choosing where to situate your machine. Besides setting up on a subway or busy street, you can choose to operate your machine from an office park, hotel or restaurant, or a nearby college or university. Operators who seek to remain competitive may even choose to invest in intelligent vending machines with integrated voice recognition technology and cashless systems.

With the global and domestic economy steadily recovering from losses due to the pandemic, vending machine businesses are working at full steam and the industry is expected to rebound with full force. Hence, this is a sweet time for all those who want a steady passive income to enter the industry and start their own vending machine business.

The Benefits of Starting a Vending Machine Business

It is difficult to ignore the benefits of starting a vending machine business. Very few business models will deliver low startup costs, flexibility, and potentially high growth potential. The fact that there are millions of machines in the U.S. alone should be enough to convince you that there is a gap in the market for your business. Below are the most attractive benefits of starting a vending machine business:

1. Low Initial Investment

To get started, you will need to buy or lease a vending machine, and have enough funds to stock your machine with goodies. However, apart from that, your machine will require little human effort and maintenance. Unlike a traditional restaurant or convenience store, you won't need to hire staff to manage your machine. Having very low overhead reduces your startup costs significantly, which allows you to invest money in other aspects of your business, like marketing.

2. Adaptable to Changing Technological Landscape

Modern technology is changing how many businesses operate. Fortunately, it is very simple for vending machine businesses to adapt to changing consumer demands as a result of new technologies, like cashless payments. All it takes is finding a supplier who sells intelligent vending machines. The technology comes already built-in, so you won't need to worry about developing your own systems.

3. Revenue Isn't Limited to Certain Times of the Day

Traditional retail stores have operating hours in which consumers can purchase goods. Vending machines are unique because they are fully operational 24/7, as long as there are products to be sold. This means that consumers can purchase from your vending machine during and outside traditional working hours, including days like Sundays or public holidays when traditional stores would be closed.

4. Requires Minimal Maintenance

You will often hear people referring to the vending machine business as a form of passive income. The reason they say this is because managing a machine doesn't require a lot of your time or energy. Once your machine has been installed, you will only need to check in once or twice a week to replenish stock and collect money. If you have ticked these boxes and everything is operating as normal, you won't need to do anything else.

5. Variety of Products to Sell

There is no one-size-fits-all approach when choosing what to sell
in your vending machine. Each business owner gets to select
goods that are most suitable to their chosen target market and
geographical location. For example, a vending machine situated
at an office park might do well selling hot coffee on-the-go,
whereas a vending machine situated at a hotel lobby might do
well selling a variety of snacks and beverages. In more recent
years, there has been a push for healthy foods and beverages.
This has been the result of diets like veganism, gluten-free, or
keto gaining popularity. Business owners can capitalize on these
trends and cultural movements when thinking about what to
stock in their machines.

The Challenges of Starting a Vending Machine Business

With every reward comes a certain amount of risk. Like any
other business, there are downsides that business owners may
experience when starting up. These downsides may be related to
sourcing funds, finding the right customers, or deciding on the
right products. If you do not anticipate these challenges, you
will not be able to address them from the onset. Here are a few
common challenges to note:

1. The Bigger the Enterprise, the More Profits

A typical vending machine makes around $300 per month. Some
vending machines that are not situated in prime locations, or
sell the wrong products, make far less than that. What this
means is that your business is unlikely to profit from a single
machine. If you want to eventually leave your 9-to-5 job and
survive on the profits generated by your business, you will need

to plan on scaling your business and slowly adding more machines.

2. Tough Competition for Prime Locations

Due to how little profits a single machine generates, business owners compete on finding the best locations to install their machines, in order to receive more foot traffic. Research shows that locations frequently visited by blue-collar workers are more profitable since they are likely to buy twice as many vending machine products (Gleeson, 2019). However, even in these prime locations, it can be difficult to find an area that isn't already saturated with vending machines.

3. Small Added Expenses Can Pile Up

It is important to factor every fixed and variable expense your vending machine may accrue. Some of the smaller expenses that are overlooked are licensing and permit fees, electricity to power the vending machine, and insurance coverage. When creating your startup budget, take note of these expenses to avoid running into unexpected costs later on.

4. Investing in the Wrong Product

Finding the right location is crucial, but so is investing in the right product. Avoid selling products that are not in demand or sought out by your typical customer. Your machine should respond to their existing needs, rather than seek to push them out of their comfort zones. For example, if your typical customer is more driven to purchase grab-and-go snacks from a vending machine, avoid selling ready-made meals or other packaged foods. The concept of buying a meal from a vending machine may be foreign to them, or they may have concerns about the freshness of the products. It is therefore too much of a gamble to introduce them to products they would not typically purchase.

5. Risk of Theft and Vandalism

Vending machines are vulnerable to theft and vandalism, especially newer models of machines (as compared to older or used machines). Choosing the right location can protect business owners from these kinds of threats, but there is no guarantee that theft or damage will never happen. By investing in insurance coverage, businesses can protect themselves in the event of these situations occurring.

THE BUSINESS PROPOSITIONS

Earlier on, I mentioned the concept of a vending machine business model. A business model is simply the company's formula for generating revenue. Generally speaking, the business model for a vending machine business involves finding a great spot to install a machine, so target consumers can purchase products for sale.

However, as we get more technical, we will see that there are three types of business models that vending machine business can adopt. The choice of which model to pick depends on the owner's goals, available funds, and whether they want to be involved on a full-time or part-time basis. Below is a breakdown of each model and the advantages and disadvantages of each:

Model 1: Set Up Your Vending Machine Business From Scratch

Choosing to establish your own vending machine business can seem like taking the longer route, but it can provide you with more flexibility in the long run. When you are the person in charge of your business, you get to decide on the business strategy, expansion plans, branding, and customer sales experience.

The advantages of using this model are:

- You can design your business to your liking, including what the name will be, where you will operate, and what products to sell.
- You can control your startup expenses by monitoring your budget and finding ways to reduce overhead costs.

The disadvantages of using this model are:

- You will need to invest a lot of your time setting up the business and making sure it is fully operational and profitable.
- You must have good selling and negotiation skills to find the right suppliers, negotiate deals on locations, and make potential customers aware of your business.

This type of model often terrifies aspiring business owners the most because of how risky it seems. Fortunately, this book has been written from the perspective of this model, so you will receive plenty of guidance on how to get your vending machine business up and running in record-breaking time!

Model 2: Buy a Vending Machine Franchise

The second type of model involves buying a vending machine franchise. This model is great for investors who desire to buy into a business that has proven to generate revenue and already has a loyal customer base. Essentially, all they need to do is follow the existing blueprint to make their business a success.

There are a number of advantages of using this model, such as:

- Most franchises offer franchisee support and training throughout the process, including guidance on how to pick the right location, implementing an effective marketing strategy, and where to source affordable products.
- Since you are buying a ready-for-market startup model, you can save a lot of time on doing market research, building a brand, or formulating winning business strategies. All of the supporting documents you will need to run your business are handed over to you.

Nonetheless, this model isn't for every business owner, and it can come with a few disadvantages too, such as:

- Buying an existing franchise requires a large sum of capital.
- Some franchises may require a commission from every sale, or might charge monthly or yearly licensing or maintenance fees.

This model typically works well for investors who have little to no time establishing a business. Their main goal is making profits, not necessarily building a brand or community around their business. Therefore, this option takes much of the work of setting up a business off their shoulders.

Model 3: Buying an Existing Vending Machine Business

The third model offers the best of both worlds. It offers you an opportunity to invest in a business with proven profitability, but gives you the freedom to rebrand and make it more successful, using your own sales and marketing strategies.

If you look online, you will always find businesses for sale. Owners choose to sell businesses for many reasons, such as lack of cash flow, early retirement, or the desire to invest in other assets. Buying an existing vending machine business can save you time on building your own from scratch.

Some of the advantages of this model include:

- The flexibility of taking on from the current owner and looking for new ways of making the business profitable.
- If you are buying an insolvent business, you can evaluate the current owner's mistakes and adopt processes to turn the business around.

However, there are also disadvantages to using this particular model, such as:

- You may be buying into a business that is in worse condition than you think, and thus may be more expensive to turn around.
- You will need to have a lot of experience recovering poor-performing businesses, or hire people who are skilled in rescuing businesses.

9

On the surface, this option may look like a golden opportunity; however, it's important to do your research and analyze the company's financial statements before signing on the dotted line. If you are not skilled at analyzing company books, hire a certified appraiser to assess the value of the business on your behalf.

Questions to Ask When Buying a Franchise or Existing Business

If you decide on buying a franchise or buying an existing business, you will need to ensure the business model you are buying into is legal and profitable. When meeting with the franchise or business owner, present questions about different aspects of the business to assess whether you are getting your money's worth. Below are just a few questions to add onto your list:

Why does the owner want to sell their business?

There could be good or bad reasons behind the sale of the business. Even though some failing businesses can be rescued with the right strategy and resources, some may be too expensive to recover.

Where are the current vending machines located?

An honest franchise or business owner will be happy to take you on site so you can see where the operating vending machines are located. While on your visit, assess the business of the area, how many pedestrians or workers walk past, and the condition of every machine. You can even visit each location during different times of the day to get a feel of how much foot traffic the machines receive.

Does the franchise or business have up-to-date tax and financial records?

It's important to ensure the franchise or business you are buying into complies with tax regulations and has at least 3–5 years worth of financial statements you can evaluate. Doing this will show you whether the sale price is worth the business valuation, and how quickly you will start making profits.

Are there any complaints filed against the franchise or business?

The franchise or business owner may not disclose if there have been any complaints filed against their companies. Therefore, as part of your due diligence, run a Google search of the franchise (or check out their social media page, if they have one), and see what comes up. You can also visit the Better Business Bureau website and check whether there are any existing and repetitive complaints. Using the Better Business Bureau tool is completely free!

Is the business willing to provide you with a Clearance Letter?

A Clearance Letter is a document showing any outstanding taxes owed by the business. Ideally, there should be no outstanding taxes, although if there are, you can calculate how much they will affect your bottom line.

Is the franchise or business owner willing to stick around and help you through the transition?

The upside of buying a franchise is that you have access to a team of sales reps who can help you get your business off the ground. However, if you are buying an existing business, the current owner may not stay around to help you with transition tasks. If you are looking for this type of support, put it in writing in your legal agreement, and negotiate on the length of the transitional period.

Many aspiring investors and startup entrepreneurs have been hesitant to invest capital in businesses due to socio-economic instability brought about by the pandemic. However, the vending machine industry has remained resilient through these turbulences, and this is evident in the number of success stories shared by business owners.

Take for example the story of Jaime Ibanez. After completing high school in 2018, he used $2,500 of his savings to buy a secondhand snack machine. He installed it inside a local barbershop in Dallas, and four years later, he is the proud owner of 35 machines that bring in a total of $10,000 every month.

A private Facebook group called VendingNation saw an increase of members during January 2020. The group grew from roughly 6,000 members to 14,500 members. Many of the new members were people seeking to make extra income during the pandemic. Since the vending machine model is recession-proof and requires very little human contact, many saw it as a great business to enter during the lockdown.

Jalea Pippens, who bought her first machine during lockdown, was astounded at the amount of revenue she and two partners (her boyfriend and best friend) were able to make. In less than a year, they were able to purchase 14 more machines, bringing the total to 15, and installed them in various locations around Metro Detroit. In total, their machines generate a total of $4,000 in revenue, every month.

Which factor inspires you the most to start your own vending machine business? Keep reading further, as you will learn what it takes to become the next success story if you follow what's written in this book.

Now that you have an idea of the size, value, and potential opportunities of the vending machine industry, let's probe deeper into understanding the market.

CHAPTER 2
SCRATCHING THE SURFACE

VENDING MACHINES IN THE POST-COVID ERA

The retail industry will continue to experience shifts due to the nature of consumer needs in a post-Covid era. Now more than ever, consumers are concerned about the health and hygiene of retail facilities. Buying products from vending machines has gained appeal because it requires very few touch points.

The World Health Organization (WHO) has emphasized the need for contactless and cashless payments. This trend had already been set in motion in the vending machine industry prior to the pandemic. Currently, over half of all vending machines in the United States accept cashless payments, meaning consumers can simply insert or tap their credit cards, and go.

The shift from cash to cashless has also positively affected the bottom line. Findings from the *Intelligent Vending Technology in the U.S.: Reinventing an Industry* report showed that after converting to cashless payments, sales increase between 10—35% per machine, and low-performing machines (those that generated less than $2,000 yearly) experience a sales growth of 110% over 18 months, after adopting a cashless payments system (PaymentsJournal, 2019).

KNOW YOUR MARKET

The vending machine market can be divided into various market segments, such as product type, application, and technology. For instance, when categorizing machines based on product type, you can find snack machines, beverage machines, tobacco machines, and so on. There are some products, like beverages, that are more profitable than others. In 2019, beverage machines generated the most revenue, subsequently taking up the largest market share. What makes beverage machines so popular and profitable is the fact that they can be installed in a variety of locations.

Another common way to categorize vending machines is to think about where they are more likely to be used. In the previous chapter, we read the story of Ibanez who installed his first machine in a local barbershop. This would be considered an unconventional spot since many of us wouldn't think of placing a vending machine in a barbershop. However, upon further analysis, it makes perfect sense why customers would want to buy snacks or drinks while waiting for a haircut.

Hotels and restaurants were seen to be the most popular spots to install vending machines in 2019 because these locations catered to a large consumer base. Other factors influencing the popularity of hotels and restaurants for vending machines is the rise in tourism and fine dining. Vending machines can also be categorized based on technology, such as whether a machine is automatic, semi-automatic, or an intelligent machine.

GETTING CREATIVE: UNIQUE IDEAS FOR YOUR VENDING MACHINE BUSINESS

If you still believe that consumers go to vending machines looking for conventional snacks and beverages, think again. Why would they purchase snacks from a vending machine that they could potentially find cheaper somewhere else?

What many consumers are looking for are niche products that can't be found anywhere else. Think CBD-infused beverages, portable travel chargers, or cupcakes. There is no limit to how wild your imagination can travel, as long as you respond to the needs of your target market.

Here are a few crazy vending machine ideas inspired by real-life, profitable vending machines:

Crab vending machine: Crab meat is a delicacy in Asia, particularly in China and Hong Kong. It is therefore not shocking that crabs are not only sold in supermarkets, but can be bought from a vending machine at a subway station. The machine stocks live, hairy crabs, on a daily basis, and sells each for around $3.27, along with condiments to add when cooking.

Cupcake vending machine: If you visit Beverly Hills, California, you will likely walk past a "Cupcake ATM", a vending machine designed and operated by Kratom Crazy Sprinkles that sells cupcakes. The machine can hold as many as 600 fresh cupcakes, packaged in boxes.

Pizza vending machine: During lunch, or in between running errands, the typical consumer doesn't want to stand in long takeout queues to buy food. Fortunately, in Italy, consumers can buy hot pizza on the go with just a push of a button. The machine called "Let's Pizza" can make 100 freshly prepared pizzas from scratch (including the pizza dough).

Champagne vending machine: Some companies who seek to differentiate themselves in the beverages segment choose to sell alcoholic beverages. One company in particular, Moët et Chandon, sells mini champagne bottles on-the-go. Of course, in keeping with the brand, the machine looks elegant, and can be found inside high-end retail stores, like Selfridges in London.

Contraceptive vending machine: This type of machine might raise eyebrows for some, but students at Shippensburg University in Southampton find it rather useful. Not only does the machine sell "morning after pills," it also sells condoms, pregnancy tests, and decongestants. This institution is known as one of the best education centers in the U.S, and having this kind of vending machine available for students promotes good health.

From the examples given above, which type of vending machine attracted you the most? And why do you think that is? Even though these vending machines cost a lot of money to design, you can be inspired by the out-of-the-box solutions they each offer. You can implement an out-of-the-box solution on a small scale, and work your way to the top!

Later on in the book, we will take a closer look at different types of products to sell. For now, it's time to tackle a major factor in the success of your vending machine business—finding the right location. Let's find out how you can find that perfect spot for placing your vending machines.

CHAPTER 3
SCOUTING AROUND FOR THE PERFECT SPOT

FOLLOW THE FOOT TRAFFIC

Foot traffic is measured by the number of people who walk past a certain area, at any given time. For vending machine businesses, which rely on people visiting machines, it is important that they are installed in areas with a lot of foot traffic. This doesn't mean they should be installed on a street. Places like office parks, schools, and restaurants receive a lot of foot traffic too.

In general, 25–50 people walking past a day is considered good foot traffic. However, if you intend on generating a lot of revenue from your machine, you will need upwards of 100 people walking past your machine every day.

School teacher Barry Strickland, and his wife, Lory, started their vending machine business in the 1980s, with five machines. By the time they sold their business, they owned 250 machines located across the San Diego area. Today, they provide maintenance services for old machines and run courses to educate aspiring entrepreneurs seeking to start vending machine businesses.

One of the lessons they teach entrepreneurs is how to find locations with a lot of foot traffic. Contrary to what many entrepreneurs believe, white-collar offices and upmarket hotels and restaurants are not great spots to install vending machines. Consumers with a lot of spending power typically won't choose to buy products from a vending machine—they would rather pay a premium for quality elsewhere. It is mostly blue-collar workers and businesses that support vending machines the most, while also providing the most foot traffic. Therefore, when looking for potential spots, Barry and Lory suggest areas where workers are doing a lot of physical labor (i.e. construction sites), nursing homes, schools and universities, and express hotels and motels (i.e. places where guests are likely to skip meals).

HOW DOES LOCATION AFFECT PROFITS?

When it comes to films, the secret to success is entertainment. But in the vending machine business, the secret to success is location! Where you install your vending machine has a direct correlation to your potential revenue. For example, if you placed a machine in an area with less than 25 people walking past every day, you probably wouldn't make as much money as you would if it were placed inside a busy shopping mall.

Foot traffic isn't the only "location factor" that affects profitability. Here are a few more factors to consider when choosing the perfect location to install your first machine:

1. Expensive Locations

Business owners face a common dilemma when looking for areas to install their machines. The locations where there is extremely high consumer demand are usually the most expensive to rent. Since the margins per machine are relatively low, renting an expensive location can affect the profitability of your business, even if customers are purchasing your products. Ideally, the right location will minimize overhead and maximum income.

2. Picking the Right Target Market

Locations are often populated with different demographics of people. Upmarket suburbs, streets, and restaurants are likely to attract middle to upper class consumers who have a lot of spending power and desire premium products and services. If you are drawn to this target market, be inspired by the high-end vending machines designed by Moët et Chandon and the Kratom Crazy Sprinkles cupcake company. However, if your target market is students, office workers, or manual laborers, you will need to find locations where they are more likely to visit often.

3. Competition

Sometimes, a location isn't right because there are just too many direct competitors operating there. Direct competitors are companies that sell similar products or services, and hope to attract a similar target market. The only advantage when it comes to competitors is operating near indirect competitors. These are companies who operate in the same industry but sell different products or services, and serve a different target market. Being around indirect competitors can boost your sales since you can draw twice as many customers.

4. Suppliers and Employees

Another factor to consider is the distance between your suppliers and the location of your machine. The farther away your machine is, the more expensive it will be to source and transport products. Moreover, if you are planning on hiring employees to manage your machine (although this won't be necessary), you would also need to think about how far your machine is to public transport systems.

BEST LOCATIONS FOR INSTALLING VENDING MACHINES

When selecting the best location for your vending machine, remember this rule: If people cannot see it, then it probably isn't generating money. Of course, this doesn't apply to areas where vending machines are not permitted. For example, you can't install a machine on somebody else's property, or use their water or electrical connections without entering into a contract (getting written permission).

For some lucky owners, signing these contracts will be a smooth process, but for others, it could prove to be a stressful exercise! Other nearby buildings or restaurants will want a cut from your earnings, and these negotiations can be what take up most of your time. However, once your paperwork is in order, you shouldn't experience any more hassles from your 'landlords'.

So, what are some of the best locations to check out when deciding on where to install your vending machine? Here are a few options to consider:

1. Manufacturing Facilities

Manufacturing facilities include industrial parks, warehouses, and distribution centers. These areas tend to attract hundreds of people on a daily basis, who typically work around the clock (each entering at different shifts). Since manufacturing facilities aren't exactly close to any retail stores, workers often bring packed lunches, or buy food from food trucks and vending machines during their breaks.

2. Office Parks

Another great location is office parks. What makes them a prime spot for vending machines is that they attract hundreds of professionals on a daily basis, and the corridors inside the building lend themselves to vending machines. Quick and easy-to-eat snacks and beverages work best in this environment because they provide a quick snack to keep workers energized.

3. Apartment Buildings

An apartment building may not be the first or second location that comes to mind when choosing the best vending machine spots. However, the appeal is similar to a hotel or motel with a vending machine—except these are not guests; they are long-term tenants. Here, you could offer more than snacks and beverages. For instance, you could stock products that residents usually buy at the local gas station, like tobacco, cosmetics, newspapers and magazines, and so on.

4. Hospitals

Hospitals receive a lot of foot traffic. There are hundreds of nurses and doctors that work around the clock, as well as friends and family that stay long hours visiting their loved ones. Once again, besides the conventional snack and beverage machine, you can be creative and think of other products that people would need at a hospital. For example, what if they forgot their phone charger at home? They would certainly buy a travel charger from your vending machine. Another facility that we can add under this category is a nursing home.

5. Hotels and Motels

During the night, or early in the morning, when dining options are few, many hotel and motel guests make their way to the vending machine. It is cheaper than ordering room service or going out of the establishment to buy food. Vending machines also tend to be installed off the passageway, along with the ice machine. Therefore, many guests are likely to walk past the vending machine whenever they are getting ice, or perhaps using the exit doors. Other spots for installing vending machines are the hotel lobby and the underground parking lot.

6. Gyms

If you go to the gym a lot, you will notice how hungry you feel after your workout. Burning all of those calories causes you to work up an appetite. Vending machines located in gyms often stock energy drinks, healthy snacks, and other accessories that members may have forgotten at home, like a disposable towel or water bottle.

7. Schools, Colleges, and Universities

Students who forget their lunch at home or feel like snacking during or after school hours tend to flock to the vending machine. This is especially true in schools where there is no cafeteria—or when the cafeteria food is not free. Parents and teachers will want to ensure that the products sold in the vending machine are priced for students and are mostly healthy. Colleges and universities will offer you more flexibility in terms of what you can sell to students, and how much to price your goods. You can also consider college dorm rooms or other types of student accommodation when looking at your options.

8. Laundromat

Local laundromats are another great spot to install vending machines because they receive a lot of foot traffic, and some customers will hang around and wait for their laundry. Once again, you can offer unconventional products inside your vending machine, such as laundry powder, fabric softeners, stain removers, and so on.

USING A LOCATOR SERVICE

To help you in your search for the best location to install your vending machine, you can hire a locator service. Approach reputable companies that have positive reviews and a proven track record of finding locations that cater to your budget. Some companies will go as far as speaking to site owners or managers on your behalf and pitching the idea of having a vending machine in their premises.

However, all of this comes at a charge. It's important to ensure that you are getting value for your money. Avoid approaching locator services that don't conduct market research prior to searching for the best locations. And even when they find a location, it's important for the agent to understand the costs of running your machine at that place. For instance, they should be able to tell you how much your overhead will cost per month, and if there are any permits you need to obtain before setting up your machine.

If hiring a locator service is out of your budget, you can also take the hands-on approach and find suitable locations on your own. Don't worry, you don't need to have a real estate license to do this.

For instance, if you can find a business park that is a new building or still under construction, you may have found your pot of gold! Ideally, you want to be one of the first vending machine businesses to pitch to the developers or site manager, and give them a good offer. To stay updated on new companies setting up in your city, you can join business organizations or frequently read your local newspaper.

You can also schedule appointments with local property developers. Property developers are often in charge of managing new residential and commercial buildings. If you are looking to install your vending machines in apartment complexes, pitch your business to developers and explain the benefits of having fully stocked and regularly maintained vending machines in their apartment complexes. If there are any apartments you have already identified as being a great fit for your business (perhaps members of your target market reside in those buildings), explain where your vending machine would sit, the type of products you would stock, and how frequently you would check on your machine.

Another great way to find a location for your vending machine is to put yourself in your customers' shoes. Think about the places you often see vending machines, what you normally purchase from a vending machine, and whether other factors play a role, such as the time of day, how much money you have on you, or whether it is a matter of convenience (eg. It is easier to grab your coffee at your office vending machine than walk a block to the nearest coffee shop).

Have you narrowed down the potential locations yet? If you haven't, feel free to take your time. Committing to a location is costly and you want to make sure you are making a good decision. After you have locked down the location for your vending machine, you will have to figure out what kind of products to offer customers, and why.

CHAPTER 4
CHOOSING THE RIGHT PRODUCT MIX

WHEN PRODUCTS SEND THE WRONG MESSAGE

After the release of a 2015 survey completed by hospital trusts in England, there was public outrage about the products stocked in NHS hospitals. Citizens were shocked to find out that most hospitals sold sugary snacks and beverages in their vending machines, rather than healthy and fresh products.

Tam Fry, the spokesperson for the National Obesity Forum, said that NHS hospitals were sending the wrong message, particularly about the seriousness of chronic diseases like diabetes and obesity. Since the release of the survey, public hospitals in England are working toward improving the quality of products stocked in vending machines that are offered to staff, patients, and visitors.

CHOOSING THE RIGHT PRODUCTS

There are three categories of vending machines that you can choose from. These are food and beverage machines, bulk machines, and speciality machines. The machine you select will guide you on the type of products to stock. In this section, we will explore two categories of machines—food and beverage machines and specialty machines—and look at the variety of products to sell.

Popular Foods and Beverages for Your Vending Machine

The first vending machine you probably laid your eyes on was a machine selling snacks and beverages. This type of machine is the most popular and makes up the largest market share. As a first-time vending machine owner, you can't go wrong investing in one of these machines because you are guaranteed to find customers looking to buy confectionery snacks and beverages. However, be careful not to make the same mistake that NHS hospitals did and stock inappropriate products for your target market or location.

When it comes to selecting a range of snacks, note that consumers have different preferences. Some may love sugary snacks, while others prefer more salty or spicy savory treats. It is therefore important to include a wide variety of options that consumers can choose from. According to research from 360Connect, the following snacks are the most popular for vending machines nationwide (Catie, 2020):

- **Snickers bars:** According to research, Snickers bars are the most popular vending machine snack in the United

States. In 2012, NBC News named the Snickers bar as America's favorite chocolate brand, grossing more than $400 million in sales each year (Bottom Line, 2012).

- **Clif bars:** These energy bars can be eaten as a breakfast or midday snack, and provide more nutritional value than chocolate bars. Clif bars also come in many different flavors, such as chocolate brownie, blueberry crisp, crunchy peanut butter, and white chocolate Macadamia nut.

- **Pop-tarts:** Another great breakfast snack option to stock in your vending machine are pop-tarts. They are affordable, delicious, and come in many different flavors. According to consumer reviews, the most popular pop-tart flavors are "Brown Sugar Cinnamon", "Blueberry", and "Frosted Strawberry" (Koman, 2019).

- **Sun chips:** When it comes to potato chips, one of the popular brands sold in vending machines are Sun chips. These are often bought as a lunchtime snack, paired with just about anything. Compared to other potato chip brands like Lays, Sun chips come in more flavors, are lower in fat, and are 100% whole grain.

- **Reese's peanut butter cups:** Reese's is a popular American candy brand sold in vending machines nationwide. One of the top-selling products offered by the brand are the peanut butter cups. These are simply chocolate cups filled with peanut butter, in packs of 2, 4, 5, 10, or 20.

- **Granola bars:** If you are looking for versatile snacks, granola bars are another consumer favorite. They are delicious and pack plenty of nutritional value. Fortunately, there are many great brands to choose from

when selecting granola bars, such as Nature's Valley,
Chewy granola bars, and Kind bars.

- **Chex mix:** These are a great option when looking for
  salty snacks to add to your vending machine. They
  contain less calories than potato chips and offer a variety
  of flavors, all in one packet!
- **Pretzels:** On the subject of salty snacks, pretzels are
  another American favorite. Compared to other savory
  snacks, they have fewer calories and are a good source
  of energy. Once again, there are many great pretzel
  brands to choose from, such as Goldfish Pretzels,
  Snyder's, or Rold Gold.

Now that you have a decent list of snacks to choose from, you
will need to select some beverages to offer consumers.
Compared to other vending machine products, beverages
generate the most revenue, making up about 31% of vending
machine purchases each year. Similar to snacks, you will need to
ensure that your beverages selection includes a wide range of
options, such as sugary and sugar-free drinks, or caffeinated and
decaffeinated drinks. According to research from 360Connect,
here are the most popular beverages to sell in your vending
machine:

- **Bottled water:** This is a standard product that every
  machine must include when offering beverages. There
  are many consumers who buy bottled water throughout
  the day to stay hydrated. You can choose whether you
  want to add a variety of water brands or stock flavored
  and carbonated water.
- **Energy drinks:** There are some consumers who are

looking for an energy boost during the day. Energy
drinks can be a great pick-me-up, and appeal to people
who are not coffee drinkers. Not all energy drinks are
dangerous for your health. If you are looking for
healthier energy drink brands, consider Zevia Energy,
Matchabar Hustle, or Yerbamate.

- **Cold coffee:** If you are appealing to coffee lovers, selling
cold coffee can be a great way for them to get their
caffeine fix during the day. It is a great beverage to enjoy
on the go and provides a quick boost of energy. Cold
coffee can also come in delicious and exotic flavors that
your customers will love.
- **Sodas:** How can we complete the list of beverages
without adding sodas? Even though many people are
now health conscious and look for alternatives to sodas,
these beverages still make a lot of money in vending
machines. A poll by Gallup showed that 50% of
Americans drink soda at least once every day
(MyHealthNewsDaily, 2015). There are many different
types of sodas to choose from; however, the most
popular brands are Pepsi, Coca-cola, Dr. Pepper, Sprite,
and Mountain Dew. It is also good to include diet or
sugar-free sodas for customers looking for healthier
alternatives.

Alternative Healthy Options to Consider

We cannot deny the global move to healthier food and beverage
products. Due to the rising cost of healthcare and efforts to eat
and live healthier, consumers are constantly on the hunt for
products with higher nutritional value. If you decide to go the

healthy route, you will need to research the types of products you are offering and ensure they are sourced, prepared, and packaged in an environmentally-friendly and health-conscious manner. In general, select products that have labels like organic, 100% natural, vegan, gluten-free, preservative-free, lactose-free, and so on.

Below are lists of healthy food and beverage options to consider:

Healthy Snacks

- jerky
- raisins
- trail mix
- energy bars
- applesauce

Healthy Beverages

- water
- iced tea
- lemonade
- 100% Fruit and vegetable smoothies
- protein shakes

Healthy product vending machines tend to also offer healthy on-the-go meals, ranging from breakfast muesli to wholesome dinner options. These pre-packaged meals cater to people who want to grab a quick breakfast, lunch, dinner, or post-workout meal. Here are a few options when stocking healthy meals:

- oatmeal

- muesli
- noodle dishes
- soups
- rice dishes
- quinoa

Expanding on healthy products even more, some vending machines go as far as adding wellness products to their product list. Wellness products are a category that is growing in popularity. During the pandemic lockdown, consumers turned to vending machines when buying over-the-counter medication, personal care products, or popular supplements because of the limited access to traditional retailers. Some of the popular wellness products stocked in vending machines include:

- toothbrush and toothpaste
- deodorants and lotions
- hand sanitizers
- over-the-counter medications
- essential oils
- face masks and shields

Specialty Products for Your Vending Machine

Rather than selling food and beverages, you may be interested in selling specialty products. These are niche products such as travel items, clothing, beauty accessories, specific foods or cuisine, or tech accessories. These products are typically targeted to specific customers, in very specific locations. Below are a few examples of specialty products you can sell in your machine:

- **Frozen desserts:** If you are appealing to customers with a sweet tooth, you can purchase a custom vending machine built to sell frozen desserts. An example of this is Vending.com's Frozen Treat's Ice Cream machine that allows you to add up to 36 selections of desserts and 540 products in total.

- **Laundry products:** One of the prime locations to install your vending machine is inside a local laundromat. Some of the special products you could offer include mini detergents, fabric softeners, and cleaning products.

- **Sanitary products:** In manufacturing facilities or business parks, where there are many people walking in and out each day, offering sanitary products can be a great way to promote hygiene and keep consumers safe. Examples of sanitary products you can offer include face masks, hand sanitizers, disinfectant wipes, and disposable hand gloves.

- **Tobacco products:** While there are a multitude of health hazards that come with smoking, many consumers continue to support the tobacco industry. Cigarettes and other related tobacco products are among the most profitable to sell in a vending machine, due to the high demand. Examples of popular tobacco products include cigarettes, cigars, hookah coal or flavor, chewing tobacco, and lighters.

FACTORS AFFECTING THE PRODUCT MIX

Selecting your assortment of products isn't as easy as picking the most affordable or highly-sought-after products. Your product range will be influenced by a number of factors, such as:

1. Price

To maximize profits per product sold, you will need to ensure that every item positively impacts your business's profitability. In other words, you should be able to add a reasonable margin on every product. The best way to do this—without raising the sale price—is to source affordable products that you can buy in bulk. The lower the cost price, the higher the margin you can add on each product.

2. Customer Demand

It's also important to conduct market research and investigate what kinds of products your target market frequently purchases from vending machines. Ideally, you want to stock products that are in high demand and can be bought on a recurring basis. You can also measure demand by taking note of how often you restock certain products. Those that are typically out of stock within a week are your most in-demand products, and others that remain untouched for months have less of a demand.

3. Government Laws and Bans

Read about the local and national laws and bans about products to stock in your vending machine. If you are found selling products that are banned or illegal, you may be fined by authorities. It is also worth reading about the industry's competition laws, like how much distance there needs to be between direct competitors.

4. Taste

The advantage of sourcing recognizable branded products is that customers are already familiar with the taste. This leaves no room for disappointment when they purchase and consume a product. However, if you are going to stock unrecognizable brands, ensure that it meets your customers' taste preferences. Run a focus group or ask members of your target market to complete a survey evaluating the taste of certain products you wish to sell. It may help if your products taste similar to well-known branded products.

5. Uniqueness

Since there are so many vending machines across the country, you need to ask yourself why customers would choose your particular vending machine. What is unique about the products you sell? Or what is unique about how you sell recognizable products? For example, you could offer the same range of snacks and beverages as any other vending machine in your area, but what makes your machine unique is that the products are reshuffled every week, giving customers different options to choose from. Or perhaps what makes your machine unique is the fact that you stock exotic flavors that customers can't find in retail stores.

6. Nutritional Value

Due to global health trends and the pressure on food manufacturing companies to include more diet-conscious alternatives, customers expect to see healthy food and beverage options in your vending machine. This could be as simple as including sugar-free sodas, decaffeinated coffees, and low-fat chocolate bars.

By now, I'm sure your mind is buzzing with possible product ideas. Jot some of your ideas on paper and create different food and beverage combinations. Think about which snacks, beverages, or pre-packaged meals would complement one another. Get inside your customers' shoes and consider which combinations you would most likely buy.

Once you have done your product research, the next step is selecting the best type of vending machine to arrange your products. The following chapter will help you narrow down your options when searching for the most suitable, and budget-friendly, vending machine.

CHAPTER 5
EXPLORING DIFFERENT MACHINES

HOW VENDING MACHINES CAME TO AMERICA

Currently, there are more vending machines in the U.S. than any other country in the world. Surprisingly, however, vending machines were not invented in the U.S. The first vending machine dates back over 2,000 years ago to first-century Greece. The machine was invented by an engineer and mathematician by the name of Hero of Alexandria. It was a coin-operated machine that dispensed a measure of holy water used for ritual washings in Egyptian temples.

In the 17th century, English inventors made a spin off of the coin-operated machine and installed them in pubs across England. What was sold? None other than tobacco products. Two centuries later, an English publisher named Richard Carlile created a newspaper dispensing machine where he sold banned writings. He was charmed by the contactless trading and figured local authorities wouldn't be able to trace the seller.

WALTER GRANT & MATT COLEMAN

Vending machines only arrived in the U.S. toward the end of the 19th century. Can you guess what products were sold inside the early machines?

Tutti-Frutti gum.

The first American vending machines were operated by the Thomas Adams Gum Company in 1888. They installed Tutti-Frutti gum machines on elevated subway platforms throughout New York City. In 1907, gumball dispensing machines started to pop up around the country, and this led to the experimentation of many other products that could be sold through vending machines.

Cross over to the 21st century, and we are witnessing more tech-inspired features in vending machines, such as cashless and biometric payments, voice-operated machines, and touchscreen menus. Modern vending machines are also built with more than snacks and beverages in mind. They are offering health, investment, and lifestyle products that were inconceivable many centuries ago.

The benefit of operating vending machines in the U.S. is that you get to be among the pioneers of intelligent vending machine systems, and pave the road for the rest of the world to follow!

THE DIFFERENT VENDING MACHINE OPTIONS FOR YOU

As mentioned in the previous chapter, there are three types of vending machines: food and beverage machines, bulk machines, and specialty machines. Instead of looking at the products you can stock inside these machines, we will now look at each machine and the pros and cons of operating them.

1. Bulk Vending Machines

Do you remember visiting the arcade and asking your parents for a quarter so you can buy candy from a globe-like machine? You would then take your quarter, insert it in the slot machine, and turn the lever, which would send pieces of candy running out. This type of machine is known as a bulk vending machine, and typically stocks items such as candy, small toys, or stickers.

A quarter often releases 7–10 pieces of candy to the customer. Now this may sound like a bargain, but since these items are sourced in bulk, one piece could cost the seller 2 cents from the wholesaler. The potential revenue from a bulk vending machine is not high; however, there is very minimal overhead, which makes this a great option for passive income.

A standard bulk vending machine costs between $150–$450, and the products you stock inside are normally bought in bulk and have good profit margins. And since bulk vending machines don't have motors, they won't require a lot of maintenance either, which means you will have low operational costs.

2. Food and Beverage Vending Machines

These are popular vending machines that you will find in many locations. They tend to sell confectionary goods like soda, candy, chocolates, potato chips, and other sugary treats. The cost of a standard food and beverage machine is between $1,000–$3,000 if the machine is refurbished, or between $3,000–$5,000 if the machine is brand new. It will also have higher operational costs than a bulk vending machine since an average machine is powered by electricity and may require maintenance on an ongoing basis.

However, the profit margins per product are significantly higher than products sold in bulk vending machines. For example, if you operate a bulk vending machine, you could expect to walk away with 10–20 cents on an item, but an item sold in a food and beverage machine can generate a dollar or more in profits. Of course, other factors like location and customer demand can also affect profitability.

3. Specialty Vending Machines

Specialty vending machines cater to specific target markets. They offer exclusive products that may be a little more expensive than snacks and drinks, due to their specialized nature. Moreover, specialty vending machines tend to require more customization, which makes them a lot more expensive to buy. For instance, you could find a brand new specialty vending machine in the marketplace for between $3,000—$10,000, and it is very rare to find a refurbished machine. However, if you have studied your target market well, you could make a lot of profits from selling specialty goods.

There is no preferred machine to start out with, since each machine has its pros and cons, and one might be more profitable in a certain area than another. You will also need to determine which factor is most important when buying a machine: Is it the product mix, the price of the machine, or how much it costs to operate the machine?

For instance, if you have already decided on selling healthy snacks and drinks, then the food and beverage machine is the most suitable. But if price is a major factor for you, then the bulk vending machine is the most affordable option. When purchasing a refurbished machine, bear in mind that it could cost more to repair or service, compared to purchasing a brand new machine. Research the model number of the refurbished machine and find out how much spare parts cost (and how easy it is to obtain them).

NEW VS. REFURBISHED MACHINES

As an entrepreneur, you will always look for ways to save money on startup costs when starting a business. In general, your largest expense when getting your vending machine off the ground will be purchasing a machine, which could cost upwards of $1,000. It makes sense then why you would want to get a bargain on a machine and lower your total startup costs. But is purchasing a cheaper vending machine all it's cut out to be?

Buying a refurbished machine is the more affordable option; however, since it has been used before, it could come with a lot of maintenance issues—especially in older models. As discussed in the previous section, it can be difficult to source spare parts for older machines since they are no longer being manufactured, thus the cost of maintenance is significantly higher than maintaining newer machines.

But not all refurbished machines are low quality. Some machines, particularly those made by reliable brands, have minimal wear and tear, and have been found to be reliable in the long term. Furthermore, if you are able to buy your refurbished machine from a certified technician or reseller, there is less chance of it breaking down in the near future.

When deciding between buying a new or refurbished vending machine, ask yourself the following questions:

1. Is the Machine Repairable?

There is a difference between an old machine and a refurbished machine. Refurbished machines go through several quality checks before being resold to customers. Old machines, on the other hand, are transferred from one owner to another without going back to the factory for maintenance work. Old machines are more affordable than refurbished machines, although they also come with a lot of risks.

2. Can You Source Parts Easily?

Whether you get a new or refurbished machine, you will need to schedule maintenance work every once in a while. When buying your machine, ensure you get a recognizable brand in order to make it easier to source spare parts for your machine. The harder it is for you to source spare parts, the longer your machine will be out of operation. This will ultimately affect your revenue and brand reputation.

3. Which Supplier Will You Choose?

Having trustworthy suppliers can make your business operations a lot smoother! Look for suppliers who can take care of a wide range of services, provide professional customer support, and ideally operate locally. If you have unexpected issues with your machine, you want to be able to call your supplier and have a technician visit the machine within a few hours or days. If you are buying a new machine, you will also need to find a supplier who can offer you a product warranty (the equivalent for a refurbished machine would be a parts warranty).

3. What Do Your Customers Expect?

If you are planning on installing your vending machine at an arcade or food court inside a shopping mall, your target audience won't particularly take notice of the newness of your machine. As long as it accepts cash or credit cards, and stocks the right products, they will not think less of your brand. However, if you are servicing a target market that is tech-savvy, follows trends, and supports desirable brands, the look and functionality of your vending machine will matter. Even if you can't buy a modern machine yet, branding your machine is an affordable way to make it look more attractive.

4. What Is Your Budget?

Lastly, your budget will determine whether you opt for a new or refurbished machine. Bear in mind that it is difficult to find a refurbished specialty machine. Moreover, refurbished machines may be more affordable, but their design and features are outdated. Nonetheless, starting out with a refurbished machine is a great way to get experience before investing a significant amount of money in a new model.

Entrepreneurs invest a lot of capital to start and run successful startup businesses. The best way to cut costs is to reduce expenses. If you know that your target market doesn't care much about the latest technological features in vending machines, then you don't need to invest in the latest models. A refurbished machine will get the job done at a fraction of the price.

KEY TECHNOLOGICAL FEATURES IN MODERN VENDING MACHINES

There are some customers who enjoy the experience of buying products from smart vending machines. They are followers of the latest tech trends and generally support businesses that can offer them as much convenience as possible. Fortunately, there are smart vending machines out there that make selecting and paying for products into a seamless process. Built with integrated technology, these vending machines decrease the time it takes to make purchases and ensure customers walk away feeling satisfied.

Here are some key technological features you will find in modern vending machines:

Touch interface: Includes a built-in touchscreen that is easy to navigate and maintain. Through the touchscreen, customers are able to select different quantities of products, scan their credit cards, and collect their goods.

Hybrid payment systems: Accommodates both cash and cashless payment methods for more convenience. Cashless payments are deposited to the owner's business account through direct bank transfer. If you are leasing your vending machine from a supplier, they may charge commission for every sale facilitated through their machine, while other suppliers won't.

No hassle refunds: Modern machines make it easier for your customers to request a refund, in case they face unexpected issues while ordering products.

Inventory management: With smart machines, you can track your current inventory through a dashboard at home instead of checking stock manually. This means that you only need to restock your machine when you are notified by your smart app.

Temperature regulation: Newer models of vending machines are more dynamic when it comes to temperature control. This means that you can sell both perishable and non-perishable goods without worrying about freshness.

After reading this chapter, you may have a better idea of the type of vending machine you will purchase, and whether you are going for a new or refurbished machine. The following chapter will help you start your search for the right supplier to partner with!

CHAPTER 6
FINDING THE RIGHT SUPPLIER

FINDING THE RIGHT SUPPLIER

The success of any business isn't just dependent on the product or service, but also on the consistency and reliability of its suppliers. Suppliers are the companies that provide (and transport) the products or services you need. Their reliability (or lack thereof) will impact your overall service delivery and brand reputation.

Price is not typically a leading factor when deciding on a supplier. The last thing you want is to partner with an affordable supplier who isn't trustworthy or available for customer support. In order for the union between your business and your chosen supplier to be fruitful, both of you must work together as a team. Therefore, you are looking for a supplier who will treat your business as though their success depended on it!

The right supplier will do more than just make products available. They will conduct their own market research and offer you better quality products that respond to your customers' needs, and also act as a valuable source of information when tracking competitors' actions, evaluating new opportunities, and improving marketing efforts.

The term 'supplier' is often used interchangeably with the term vendor. Even though both suppliers and vendors supply products or services, suppliers are businesses that strictly sell to other businesses, whereas vendors purchase products from manufacturers and sell to either businesses or consumers. Since suppliers sell to businesses, they often sell products in bulk quantities, while vendors sell goods in smaller quantities.

Furthermore, suppliers can be categorized into four specialty groups:

Manufacturer: A company that produces goods for sale from raw materials. They usually sell these goods to wholesalers/distributors, or hire a company salesperson to facilitate sales with various retailers. Buying directly from a manufacturer is the cheapest option since there are no middlemen.

Distributor (wholesaler): A company or independent representative that purchases goods in large quantities from different manufacturers and stores them in warehouses for resale. Although they add a margin on goods, their prices are still a lot cheaper than goods sold in smaller retail stores. They can also sell products in smaller quantities, unlike many manufacturers that enforce minimum order quantities.

Independent craftsperson: An individual (or sometimes company) that sells exotic or specialty goods to businesses catering to niche audiences. Similar to a manufacturer, they can sell through representatives or attend conferences and other trade shows. Since the goods offered are handmade or exclusive, they will cost more than goods sourced from wholesalers.

Domestic importer: A local business selling foreign goods will contact a domestic importer. This individual or company operates like a domestic wholesaler or foreign products. Buying from them will be more affordable than sourcing foreign goods on your own (and paying import duties and other taxes).

QUALITIES OF A GOOD SUPPLIER

It's good to know what to look for in a supplier before committing to any company. As mentioned before, price is not the leading factor that will determine which supplier you choose, due to other factors that could make or break your relationship. Nonetheless, ensure that your chosen supplier has fair pricing and offers benefits like discounts on certain quantities of products.

Here are a few more things you will need to ensure your supplier can offer:

1. Reliability

Can your supplier deliver quality products on time? Or do your packages take many days to arrive, or sometimes get lost in transit? When you pick up your phone and call your supplier, do they answer? Or do they have slow and unresponsive customer service? All of these scenarios are frustrating and can slow down your business. When researching suppliers, go onto their websites and assess whether they have the capacity to fulfill your weekly or monthly orders. You can also look at customer reviews and see what other businesses think about their customer service.

2. Stability

Even though you are a new business, you will need to partner with a supplier who has been in the industry for a while. They don't necessarily have to be large companies, but they must be stable and have experience catering to vending machine businesses. If your supplier isn't local, ask them about their freight policies, like shipping and import fees. Lastly, if they are importing goods from another country, they should be able to present an import license.

3. Accountability

Not every order will go smoothly. Sometimes, a package may be stolen or vandalized in transit. Other times, the quality of the products may be compromised. It's important to partner with a supplier who can admit when they have made mistakes and be accountable for the role they played in a compromised order. Not only should they take accountability, but they must also be willing to work with you to solve the issue, whether that means returning the goods, changing items, or being tighter when it comes to quality control in the future.

4. Quality

A good supplier holds themselves accountable to high standards, such as making sure they deliver quality products. In order to deliver quality products, a supplier must have a production system in place that meets your requirements. If your supplier is located nearby, you can visit their offices to verify their production capabilities and take a closer look at their systems. You can also ask the supplier about their incoming quality control, in-process quality control, as well as pre-shipment quality control. Moreover, you can have a look at the sophistication of their machinery and equipment and ask for proof of health and safety certification based on ISO 9001, or a similar standard.

5. Expertise

Since you are new to the vending machine industry, you want to partner with a supplier who can teach you more about the business and how to become more profitable. They should have experience working with other vending machine businesses or supplying similar products to other related retail businesses. The advantage of partnering with an expert is that they can easily pick up on business mistakes, such as ordering the wrong product mix, and can advise you on the best way forward.

It can be difficult to verify whether a supplier is an expert in the industry or not because the number of years they have been in the industry isn't really a good indicator of how much they know about the industry. However, you can generally see if a supplier is an expert based on the number of similar businesses they have worked with and how knowledgeable they are about your vending machine business.

SEARCHING FOR SUPPLIERS ONLINE AND OFFLINE

Before you start your search for the best supplier, you will need to be clear on what type of supplier you are looking for. Remember the four categories we discussed earlier? Manufacturers, wholesalers, independent craftspeople, and domestic importers? Well, you will need to determine which one of those suppliers can deliver the products and experience your business needs.

In general, it is recommended to search for manufacturers, so you can remove the middleman and save costs on purchasing goods. For example, if you are selling recognizable brands, it is better to purchase these products directly from the manufacturers in order to increase your margins. However, be mindful that some manufacturers enforce a minimum quantity (which may be more than you are willing to purchase at one time), and others only sell through distribution channels, like wholesalers.

Another decision you will need to make is whether to source your products locally or internationally. There are some pros and cons with both options. From a glance, sourcing your products from overseas suppliers works out cheaper, especially if your goods are produced in Asian countries, such as Taiwan, China, and India. However, since you cannot physically touch the products before receiving them, they might be of lesser quality when they arrive. Moreover, your overseas supplier's labor and manufacturing standards are specific to the laws of that particular foreign country, and may not be the same as domestic labor and manufacturing standards. This means it will be difficult to ensure quality control and that proper health and safety guidelines were followed.

On the other hand, sourcing your products locally can support the domestic economy, ensure higher manufacturing standards, and make it a lot easier to verify credible suppliers. The downside, though, is that you will pay more per unit and may be limited to the kinds of products you can purchase (there are many manufacturing products that are not made in North America). Write down a list of your manufacturing needs and determine whether it is better to contact a domestic or overseas supplier. If you end up choosing the latter, here are a few criteria for selecting a good supplier:

- Easy communication without any language barriers
- Reliable shipping (bonus for fast shipping times)
- Secure payment methods and transparent refund policy
- Proof of manufacturing certification/vendor number/sales license, etc
- Product warranty

The best place to start your search is online. Nowadays, most businesses (domestic and foreign) have a fully-functioning website, blog, or social media presence (including professional networking sites like LinkedIn). You can find a lot of information about a supplier based on what is written about them, or information they have uploaded on the internet. You will also be able to see the type of customers they have worked with, reviews and testimonials, as well as any product updates or launches.

The internet is very large, so you will need to know exactly where to source them online. Here are a few sites that you can visit:

Directories: Start your search by going onto free online directories. You will find lists of different categories of suppliers, selling various products you can stock inside your vending machine.

Search engines: Next, you can conduct a simple online search by typing in product keywords, followed by the words 'supplier' or 'wholesaler', on Google or Bing. If you are not able to find a supplier's contact details, for whatever reason, you can go onto WhoIs Lookup and type the domain name to find the website owner's details.

eBay: You can find wholesalers on sites like eBay, although bear in mind that these wholesalers may sell specialty products, and may not be able to produce high volumes of inventory. It is also possible that suppliers selling to consumers can make special orders for small businesses like yours. Reach out to as many suppliers as you can and inquire about their products and quantities.

B2B marketplaces: There are many domestic and foreign B2B online marketplaces that sell affordable products in various quantities. The largest international marketplace is Alibaba, but two large local marketplaces are Global Sources and Buyer Zone.

Industry groups and forums: Since suppliers are also businesses, they are often part of business associations and industry groups. Some of these groups require paid membership, but there are many free groups and forums on platforms such as Facebook and LinkedIn. By joining these groups you can network with various suppliers, or at the very least get trusted referrals.

Besides looking online, there are also a few ways you can meet suppliers in person. Here are some suggestions for finding suppliers offline:

Referrals: Have a look at your professional network and find business owners trading in the retail industry. Ask them where they source their products, or if they have any recommendations of reliable suppliers to contact. You can also contact industry associations, like the National Automatic Merchandising Association or the Texas Merchandise Vending Association, and ask for referrals.

Subscribe to trade publications: Find out if there are any retail magazines, newsletters, or blogs that you can subscribe to. Many of these publications attract suppliers of all kinds, plus it is a great way for you to stay updated on the latest industry trends, market research, and developments.

Attend a trade show: If you are on the hunt for new products that have just entered the market, or desire to get up close to leading manufacturers in the industry, consider attending a trade show. These networking events are great for meeting new suppliers or connecting with other business owners.

To help you get started, here are a few reputable suppliers you can contact:

- You can purchase custom vending machines through sites like Vending.com and OnlineVending.com.
- Other sites like Naturals2Go.com and eVending.com offer affordable vending machines (used and brand new), plus they can assist you with financing your machine.
- If you are looking for spare parts and accessories, visit DiscountVending.com.
- For sourcing food and beverages, you can join a

membership club, such as those offered by BJ's, Costco, and Sam's Club. You can also order your food and beverages online through e-commerce retailers like Gumball.com, Vistar.com, and Amazon Business.

If you are looking for the most reputable vending machine suppliers in the U.S, here is a top 10 list created by Thomasnet (Thomas, n.d.):

1. Mars Inc
2. Wurth Industry North America
3. Diebold, Inc
4. Crane Merchandising Systems
5. Glory, Inc
6. R.S. Hughes Co., Inc
7. Apex Supply Chain Technologies
8. Cardinal Distributing, Inc
9. Ford Gum & Machine Co., Inc
10. Betson Enterprises

DRAWING UP TERMS WITH SUPPLIERS

Before working with any supplier, there are a few questions you will need to ask to understand their business better, and whether they are a good fit for you. Below are 10 questions to ask during your first meeting; however, you are welcome to add on questions of your own:

1. What are your payment terms, and are they negotiable? As a startup vending machine business, it may take you a few months before you start making profits. Your monthly cash flow might be extremely tight, and it would be helpful to negotiate favorable payment terms with your suppliers. For example, most suppliers will expect payment within 30 days of receiving goods, but perhaps you can negotiate a 60 or 90 day repayment policy (or a discount for paying in advance).

2. Are there any additional costs you may charge? Your quote for products may not include other additional costs the supplier may later bill, such as fuel surcharges, or shipment fees. Ask your supplier to give you a list of every possible cost you may incur, and ensure that you write them down in your contractual agreement.

3. Do you have a liability insurance certificate? Your supplier should be able to present you with proof that they have coverage, in case of product or machine malfunction. This certificate is renewed yearly, so the supplier should be able to show you the most recent copy.

4. What is your return policy? Ask your supplier about their return policy, and whether they offer a guaranteed sell-through. A guaranteed sell-through makes it possible for you to return unsold products, either for a cash refund or credit.

5. What will happen if my products don't arrive on time? Late arrival of products can negatively impact your vending machine business. Ask your supplier about your options when products don't arrive on time. For instance, are you allowed to cancel the order and approach a different supplier? Or will you get a discount for the inconvenience caused? This agreement should also be in writing on your contract.

6. What is my expected gross margin? Since you will be reselling your supplier's products, ask them how much you should be selling them for. Of course, at the end of the day, the decision will be yours to make. However, it is always good to see how much a supplier thinks you should be getting on their products. If their margins are too low, it may not be a good deal to purchase a lot of their products.

7. What circumstances may cause product prices to change? Remember that suppliers are also running businesses, and their prices may change due to market supply and demand. However, other sudden changes like the rise in fuel prices or new industry regulations may affect the price of products too. Sit down with your supplier and ask them to explain factors that may affect prices, as well as when you will be notified of these changes.

8. Do you offer incentives for high volume purchases? Ask your supplier about the discounts you are eligible for, like getting products at stock price if you purchase a certain quantity. You can also negotiate the discount, if you can agree on a purchasing goal.

9. Do you have a minimum order quantity? Some suppliers, especially manufacturers, may enforce a minimum order quantity. This could be 1,000 units, a case, or a pallet of products (depending on the supplier and the goods they sell). Minimum order quantities may work in your favor because they bring the cost of goods down significantly. However, as a small business, you may not need so much inventory on hand.

10. What is your full product line? It can be a wonderful surprise to learn that your supplier offers different kinds of complementary products that you can include in your product mix. This also means that you may be able to source most of your products from one supplier, which can reduce your administrative costs and ensure you are getting the best deals on products.

Don't be shy to ask your supplier as many questions as possible. Ideally, you don't want to be caught off guard by any hidden costs or policies in the future. The transparency and accountability from the onset of your relationship will also set the tone on how you conduct business with each other.

HOW TO NEGOTIATE THE BEST DEAL

In his inaugural address, in 1961, John F. Kennedy said, "Let us never negotiate out of fear. But let us never fear to negotiate" (Good Reads, n.d.). When a supplier stipulates their terms and prices, it is never a bad thing to negotiate. You may not walk away with everything you want, but you could end up getting discounts that were not offered in your initial discussion.

As a small business owner, you are constantly looking for ways to reduce costs, and striking good deals with your suppliers is one of them. Since your relationship with your suppliers will be long-term, you should think of ways of reducing costs now, so you can save money as you grow your business.

Negotiations are not a win-lose situation. Both parties must walk away feeling as though they have benefitted from the agreement. Therefore, as much as you want to cut costs, you must also think about how your supplier can benefit. For instance, you could agree to lower prices of goods, but set a minimum order quantity to ensure your supplier makes money from each purchase too.

There are five steps involved in negotiating the best deal with your supplier, which are as follows:

Step 1: Set Objectives

When entering a purchase negotiation, you need to be clear about what exactly you want to negotiate. Remember, you may not be able to contest everything, so pick a few factors that will serve your business in the long run. Here are a few factors to consider:

- price
- delivery
- quality
- maintenance
- return policy
- payment terms

The key is to negotiate a better deal on factors that mostly influence the performance of your business. For some businesses, especially those serving discerning customers, this may not be the price, but rather the quality of the product instead. Be realistic about your expectations and remember that your supplier will want to get something out of it too.

Step 2: Think Like Your Supplier

The best way to get what you want is to offer your supplier something they want too! By thinking like them, you can structure the terms of the negotiation in a way that offers your supplier added value. By agreeing to your terms, they are essentially creating favorable outcomes for themselves too. If your supplier is a big business, it may be harder to bargain with them because they already serve many clients and may have a monopoly in the industry. Smaller suppliers who have cash flow problems or are seeking to attract more business may be a lot more flexible when bargaining.

Step 3: Create a Negotiation Strategy

Have a plan put in place before you walk into the negotiation room. Your plan must outline your objectives and the different offers you will pitch to your supplier. Moreover, be clear on what you are willing to compromise on and what you won't compromise on. This will help you steer the negotiation in a direction that favors you, and avoid being left with the short end of the stick. You will need to highlight the strengths of your partnership and why this negotiation will enhance your relations.

Step 4: Be Familiar With Negotiation Tactics

Your supplier has probably dealt with many small businesses before, which means they are aware of the negotiation process. Going into the meeting, they may even expect you to negotiate a few terms. It's important to learn common negotiation tactics your supplier might use, so you are not placed in an unfavorable position.

For example, when a supplier keeps on bringing up an urgent deadline, they could be pressuring you to make a decision on the spot. Don't allow any time constraints to force you to make quick decisions without agreeing on the terms. Or perhaps the supplier sets unreasonably high product prices so that they can offer artificial discounts during negotiations. Remember that if the price of goods isn't lower than market price, then it isn't a real discount. When it comes to price in general, never accept the first offer. Always make a counter offer and wait for the supplier to revise the price. If the price includes add-ons that you don't need, try to lower the price by asking the supplier to deduct the added features.

As you negotiate, resist the urge to be greedy. Remind yourself that your supplier is running a business, just like you, and they desire to become successful too. Negotiating terms that are unfavorable for your supplier's bottom line could ruin your entire negotiations and cause your supplier to walk away. Therefore, be fair and always aim for a win-win situation.

Step 5: Write Up a Contract

Assuming that your negotiations go well, the final step is to write up a contract to ensure that the terms you agreed upon are honored throughout the lifetime of your relationship. Written contracts provide more proof than verbal contracts, so take the time to write down every aspect of your agreement.

Ideally, your contract should protect your business interests and shift all legal responsibilities for product or machine problems to your supplier. If you are purchasing a used vending machine, for example, you would need to record any problems the machine comes with, so that if you experience any malfunctions during the product warranty period, the supplier will be responsible for repairing the fault. Your contract should also include dispute resolution processes and the exit procedure if you or your supplier are unsatisfied with your business relationship and desire to end the contract.

Have you identified a few suppliers yet? Why not run some local checks about the suppliers to begin your due diligence?

At this point, you have learned everything about the vending machine business model, including where to source your machine, how to choose the right products, and finding the perfect location. Now it's time to explore the nuts and bolts of your vending machine business, starting with understanding the basic business structure.

CHAPTER 7
IDENTIFYING THE PERFECT BUSINESS STRUCTURE

WHAT IS A BUSINESS STRUCTURE?

You are more committed to entrepreneurship now than you were at the beginning of the book. This is great news! However, you need to start thinking about the legalities of starting a business and the kind of structure your business will have.

A business structure refers to the legal entity by which the government recognizes your business. This legal entity regulates the type of relationship your business has with the government, on a federal and state level. Picking the right business structure requires more than doing a random selection. The decision is made based on several factors, such as:

- **Taxes:** Some legal entities classify their business revenue as personal income, while others are required to classify their business revenue as business income. Depending on the classification, businesses are charged different tax rates and receive different tax incentives.

- **Liability:** Depending on the business structure, owners can either separate their personal assets and debt from business assets and debt, or they are seen as being combined. If the latter is true, then it means that personal assets can be seized by the IRS or creditors to pay off business debt.

- **Hierarchy:** In some legal entities, the owner, in their capacity as the CEO, has the highest position in the company. But there are some legal entities that require a board of directors and shareholders, whom the CEO must account to.

- **Fundraising:** Some legal entities can raise funds through monies invested by shareholders, while others need to seek external funders, like banks, private investors, loan institutions, or crowdfunding sites.

- **Registration:** While every legal entity must be registered to apply for an employer identification number (EIN), the registration process, paperwork, and licenses and fees may differ for each business structure.

With these factors in mind, assessing the merits of each business structure will be a lot easier.

TYPES OF BUSINESS STRUCTURES

As a business owner, you will have the option of choosing your own business structure. You will be presented with four options, from which you can choose only one. Below is an explanation of each business structure and its unique advantages:

Sole Proprietorship

A sole proprietorship is a legal entity where an individual—the business owner—is responsible for the business profits and debts. What attracts owners to this type of structure is the fact that it is easy to set up and provides the owner with complete control. The downside with having complete control, however, is that the owner is also personally liable for any losses incurred by the business. Here are a few advantages of registering a sole proprietorship:

- **Simple setup:** There is very little paperwork involved in incorporating a sole proprietorship if you are the sole owner and there are no partners involved.
- **Low cost:** Since there is little paperwork, it is generally considered the most affordable entity to incorporate. The main costs you will need to pay are the license fees and business taxes (costs may vary depending on your state).
- **Tax benefits:** Your business may qualify for sole proprietor tax deductions, such as health deductions, depending on your business structure.
- **Hassle-free exit:** If you choose to close your business, there will be no formal paperwork required. However, you will need to ensure your taxes, business loans, and other debt is fully paid before dissolving your business.

Partnership

A partnership is a legal entity owned and managed by two or more individuals—or business owners. The owners can choose to either form a general partnership where the responsibility is shared equally, or form a limited partnership where one partner takes care of the daily operations and the other partner(s) contributes capital and shares profits. Partners can also choose how much liability to take on. They can either operate as a sole proprietorship where there is no separation between owners' and business assets, or operate as a limited liability corporation and separate their assets from business assets. Here are a few advantages of forming a partnership:

- **Simple setup**: Similar to the sole proprietorship, there is little paperwork needed to incorporate a partnership.
- **Growth potential:** Your business is more likely to have healthy cash flow since each partner contributes to the financial affairs of the business. When seeking business funding, lenders may consider two strong credit histories as being more stable, which can help you secure capital.
- **Special taxes:** General partnerships are required to file federal tax and state returns, but they are usually exempt from paying business income tax. Instead, partners will record their shared income or losses on their personal income tax returns.

Limited Liability Company (LLC)

As the name suggests, a limited liability company gives individual owners or partners the ability to separate themselves from the legal affairs of their business. The business is seen as a separate legal entity that has its own contractual obligations. Similar to partnerships, LLC's can have more than one partner, but profits and losses don't need to be distributed among partners. Below are a few advantages of incorporating an LLC:

- **Tax benefits:** An LLC is considered a pass-through entity, meaning the revenue generated by the business goes straight to its owners, without being taxed by the government. However, owners will need to declare business profits and losses on their own personal income tax returns.
- **Flexible management:** Owners can choose whether to run the business on a day-to-day basis, or to hire a professional who will manage the business on their behalf.
- **Simple setup:** The initial registration fees and paperwork required to incorporate an LLC are relatively low, although fees may vary depending on states.

Corporation

Corporations are legal entities seen as being separate from its owners. The major difference between an LLC and a corporation is the ownership. An LLC is owned and operated by a business owner, or business partners. However, a corporation is owned by its shareholders. Shareholders are investors or companies who buy a portion of a business in the form of company stocks. As the business grows, the value of their stocks grows too. The CEO of a corporation is voted in by the board of directors, who form part of the governing body of the corporation. The board of directors is responsible for making executive decisions that impact the performance of the corporation (the CEO executes the vision set by the board of directors).

There are two common types of corporations. The first is an S-corporation, which provides limited liability to the business owner, but is taxed as a partnership (as long as there are 100

WALTER GRANT & MATT COLEMAN

shareholders or fewer). The C-corporation is usually a publicly traded company that is allowed an unlimited number of shareholders, and is taxed twice: first at the company level, then secondly at the individual shareholder level. There are certain advantages of starting a corporation, such as:

- **Limited liability:** Shareholders are protected from any claims against the corporation; however, they are liable for their investment into the business.
- **Continuity:** Even when the owner leaves the business, for whatever reason, the corporation will not necessarily suffer any consequences (unlike a sole proprietorship or partnership that will be affected by the absence of members).
- **Easier to raise capital:** These types of businesses are likely to have positive cash flow due to the investments of shareholders. This makes it a lot easier to scale or expand a business when the need arises.

Out of the four business structures explained above, which business structure do you think will fit the bill for you, and why? Once you have figured out what business structure is best aligned to your objectives, it's time to get into the specifics and design a business plan that will be the blueprint you follow to run a successful vending machine business.

CHAPTER 8
DRAWING UP A PROMISING BUSINESS PLAN

ARE BUSINESS PLANS NECESSARY TODAY?

A business plan is more than a 20-page document. It is a strategic tool used by entrepreneurs to set the intention for the business and outline strategies for business success. It includes all of the large and small processes, models, and techniques that must be followed in order for the business to generate profits. A business plan not only considers 5–10 year business goals, but also clearly defines tactics on how to reach those goals.

Nowadays, when most entrepreneurs hear about a business plan, they block their ears. All they see is a waste of paper and time when creating a comprehensive business plan. However, as Benjamin Franklin once said, "If you fail to plan, you are planning to fail" (Good Reads, 2019).

In essence, the business plan is the GPS that helps you read your map (business vision), and determine the best routes to travel to arrive at your destination—which for every entrepreneur is business success. While having GPS isn't mandatory to arriving at your destination, it can shorten the length of your trip by helping you get there in the most efficient manner possible. In other words, you can start operating your business without a business plan, but you will need to figure out your strategies as you go along, which means exposing yourself to more risks and spending more money than you budgeted. Can you afford to take such risks?

Here are a few more reasons why drawing up a business plan can improve the operations of your business:

1. You can make more informed business decisions

When you draw up your business plan, you are able to look at different aspects of your business and determine the answers to some critical questions. This makes it easier for you to decide on a way forward when faced with various challenges later on.

2. You get to research the market you are entering and ensure your business solves a problem

The best businesses solve customer problems. The only way to find what problems to solve is to conduct market research and learn more about your customers' needs. In the marketing section of your business plan, you get to refine your value proposition, compare it to what your competitors are offering, and make sure your business is filling a gap in the market.

3. By planning ahead, you can avoid common startup mistakes

It is a well-known phenomenon that many startup businesses fail within three years of operation. This is due to a number of reasons, such as the business model, pricing strategy, market demand, lack of capital, or tight competition. Your business plan helps you anticipate these kinds of situations and create risk-proof strategies to reduce the likelihood of them happening.

4. Your business plan helps you provide guidelines for service providers

There are many people who you will cross paths with as you start and run your business. Some will work closely with you in your office, and others will provide services that help your business function smoothly. All of these people will need a brief or a set of guidelines to understand where they fit in, and how they can help you meet your objectives. Your business plan clearly outlines what you expect from each individual and how they fit into the bigger picture of your business.

5. You have a better chance of securing financing

When you are seeking capital for your business, lenders will often ask you to present a business plan. This is their way of making sure you have a viable business idea, and have a plan in place to generate profits.

KEY COMPONENTS OF A BUSINESS PLAN

Before you reach the stage of putting your business plan together, you have a long list of unconsolidated ideas and processes. As you complete each section of the document, you will create strategies that combine ideas and map out processes seamlessly. Each section of the document will also force you to rethink certain decisions, such as buying a new vending machine rather than investing in a refurbished one.

The length and level of detail invested into creating a business plan will differ for each business. However, in general, business plans tend to be between 15–25 pages in length. Below are the key components that every business plan should include:

1. Executive Summary

The executive summary is placed at the beginning of a business plan, even though it is often written last. Anybody who is interested in getting a brief introduction to your business can simply read this one-pager. Here, you will only touch on the key aspects of your business, such as your vision, business model, product mix, target market, and sales and marketing strategy.

2. Business Overview

When writing your business overview, think about the core values or goals that make you stand out from the rest. In this section, you will state your business name (you can provide history if you like), mission statement, core values, and any brand elements, such as logo, colors, or symbols, if you have any. The individual reading your business overview should be able to differentiate you from your competitors immediately. Therefore, avoid sounding or looking too similar to your direct or indirect competitors.

3. Products and Services

In this section, you will outline the variety of products you hope to sell in your vending machine. It's important to include the latest research on how each product sells in the market, the average cost price, and how much you plan on charging customers. If you are not selling a niche product, ensure that your individual products complement one another. For example, snacks complement beverages, but toys and beverages don't complement each other. Other information that may fit under this section include the manufacturing process (specifically the health and safety regulations you are adhering to) and a list of product suppliers who are partnering with your business.

4. Marketing

This section is one of the largest in your business plan because it consists of your market research, competitor analysis, target market analysis, as well as your online or offline marketing strategy. You can start out by giving a brief overview of the industry, then explain the gap that your business fills. You will need to prove that there is a medium to high demand for your products from the customers you hope to serve. Thereafter, you can identify a few competitors and highlight their strengths and weaknesses. Even though you may not be able to compete against their strengths, you can create strategies to outperform them on their weaknesses.

Your marketing strategy will start off with your target market analysis, which is an overview of the particular consumer segment you have chosen to sell your products. Once again, you will need to describe why you have chosen this particular segment, and why they would choose your products over direct competitors. Next, you will need to explain the step-by-step process of reaching out to your target market, online and offline, using various marketing tactics, like social media advertising, branding your vending machine, leaving flyers at a nearby office (if your machine is installed at an office park), and so on.

Include as many tactics as possible that can help you build a recognizable brand.

5. Team

As a startup entrepreneur operating one machine, you may not need a team of staff helping you run your business. As mentioned in previous chapters, you will only need to visit your vending machine once per week to collect money or restock products. However, as you grow your business and buy more machines, you will have more paperwork and systems to manage. If you still feel like you are too small to hire staff, you can purchase software that can assist you with some automated accounting or product management tasks, otherwise you can hire your first employee!

6. Finances

The final section is usually the finance section. Besides your executive summary, investors will be drawn to this section. The main objective of the finance section is to prove that you can make your business profitable in a few year's time. Even if you start with $0 in your bank account, it is important to show how having the right vending machine, in the right location, with the right products, and the right target market, can lead to generating profits.

The best way to display your financial information is by using financial statements. Since you are starting a new business, your statements will have targeted or estimated values, rather than real values. Remember to understate your income and overstate your expenses to provide the most realistic projections. If you have difficulty creating your own financial statements, you can hire the services of an accountant.

Now it's your turn. Draw up a business plan for your vending machine business! After you have created your business plan, the next step is to give your business an identity.

CHAPTER 9
NAMING YOUR BUSINESS

IN THIS CHAPTER YOU WILL LEARN:

THE IMPORTANCE OF A BUSINESS NAME

A vending machine is a vending machine. Whether it sells candy or healthy meals, most people recognize it as a vending machine. So, besides the products you sell inside your machine, what can differentiate you from other businesses?

The short answer is branding, and in this chapter, we will discuss one of the most important elements of branding—choosing the right name.

If you walked up to a bright orange vending machine with glowing letters that said "Burrito Box", what kind of product would you expect to buy? Burritos, of course! Your purchasing decision would be a quick one because the name already introduced the business and the product offering to you. The Burrito Box is a real vending machine operating in California, inside a gas station, which prepares delicious burritos on demand.

And what kind of products would you expect to buy from a vending machine called "Farmer's Fridge"? Well, you would expect to buy fresh produce or dairy products sourced from a local farm. The Farmer's Fridge, which can be found in select shopping malls around the U.S. and Canada, serves healthy meals made from scratch, and packed with as many organic ingredients as possible. Due to the name, the vending machine draws consumers who are looking for healthy alternatives to fast food.

From these two examples, you can see that there is more to a name than incorporating a legal entity. Your business name becomes the first and lasting impression you make in front of potential customers. As they walk past your machine and catch a glimpse of your name, they can make a snap judgment of whether or not to stop and take a look inside.

Here are a few benefits that come with choosing the correct business name:

1. Your name gives your vending machine an identity

A vending machine is just a piece of equipment that dispenses products. However, when you add a name to it, it takes on a personality and resonates with your customers on a deeper level.

2. It makes your business memorable

Think about how many businesses your customer comes into contact with from the time they wake up to the time they go to bed. At some point during the day, they will feel peckish or hungry. What food business will come to their mind? Ideally, you want it to be yours, but in order for that to happen, your name needs to be at the top of their mind (in marketing, this is known as brand recall).

3. Your customers can make easy referrals

When you have a catchy name that sticks in your customer's mind, they are more likely to share information about your business through word-of-mouth. For example, upon returning home from the gym, your customer might share a social media post about a product they bought from your vending machine, mentioning your name (or better yet, tagging your business) in their post. When their friends ask for referrals, your name might be the first thing that flings out their mouth, since your customers are happy to be associated with your brand.

4. It is easily discoverable on the internet. Just as much as a great business name is exciting to pronounce, it is also simple to spell and discover online. In most cases, the best names are kept short with only a few syllables. Even if the name is written in another language, it should be common enough for people to know how it is spelled.

HOW TO FIND THE RIGHT NAME FOR YOUR BUSINESS

Based on the benefits listed above, there are guidelines you can follow when thinking of a name for your business. If you have already incorporated a business name (for legal purposes), don't worry. You can create a separate brand name that is associated with your vending machine business. Think of a brand name as a mask your business wears in public, but takes off in the boardroom.

The only requirements for legitimizing this name is to either apply for a trademark, buy a domain and host a website or blog with your name, or create social media accounts with your brand name—or all of the above! Before committing to a brand name, run a trademark search and make sure there isn't another brand with the same, or similar, name. Skipping this step can lead to expensive rebranding, or in extreme cases, being sued.

Now that you know the difference between a business name and a brand name, here are a few tips on how to find the right name:

1. Create your brand identity before deciding on a name

It can be helpful to first decide on how you want customers to perceive your business before choosing a name. Based on your vision, values, and proposition, as well as the set of products you plan to sell, you may be able to think of a name that more accurately defines who you are and what you stand for.

2. Keep it short and sweet

The longer your name, the harder it is to remember. But brand recall isn't the only advantage. Shorter names perform better on Google searches because they help you stand out. For example, how much easier would it be searching for *"Candy Corner"* than it would searching for *"The Candy Corner Vending Machine Company Atlanta?"*

3. Test how easy it is to read and pronounce

Send your proposed name to a few close friends or family and ask them to rate how easy it is to read and pronounce out of a scale of 10 (1 being extremely hard and 10 being extremely easy). Chances are, if people find it easy to read your name, they will find it easy to pronounce your name too. Moreover, they won't have any trouble searching for your business online.

4. Think about the relevance of your name in the long run

It can be tempting to want to jump on a current trend or movement, and name your business after it. However, trends and movements evolve, and a few years from now, your customers may not resonate with your brand. Therefore, pick a name that can grow with your customers and remain relevant in the many years to come.

5. Incorporate popular search keywords

Many businesses overlook the importance of optimizing their name for Google searches or social hashtags. You can use an SEO tool to find a list of commonly searched words in the food and beverage industry (if you will be selling food and beverages), or any other market you will be competing in depending on your products. Thereafter, find a way of incorporating a major keyword in your name (if you can). If the keywords don't look good in your name, you can incorporate them on your blog or website, so people can easily discover your business.

6. Create a new word that is not included in the dictionary

It can be a smart move to create a new name from scratch. Not only does it make you stand out, it will make it easier to secure a domain and social media usernames. Your unique name also makes people stop and think. This is good! The more they think about you, the easier it is to remain top of mind.

After you have thought about the ideal name for your business, it is time to complete the legal paperwork. Besides incorporating a business, there are other legalities you will need to comply with, like registering for tax and securing the necessary licenses and permits. The following chapter will turn this often tedious exercise into a simple and easy-to-follow process.

CHAPTER 10
THE LAW-ABIDING
CITIZEN

REGISTERING FOR TAX

There are a host of legal formalities you will need to comply with before your vending machine business can start operating at full steam. Though often time-consuming, securing all the necessary permits and documents is essential to ensure your business avoids legal trouble.

The first thing you will need to do after incorporating your business as a legal entity is to register for tax. To do this, you will need to apply for an employer identification number (EIN). It is similar to a social security number; however, this one pertains to your business. Banks and other financial and legal institutions will ask for your EIN because it helps them ensure your business is in good standing with the IRS.

In general, sole proprietors are not mandated to have an EIN; however, in certain situations, they will need to apply for an

EIN. For instance, all businesses who meet one or more of the following criteria will need to have an EIN:

- The business hires employees.
- The business is a corporation or partnership.
- The business files excise taxes (i.e. when you are selling tobacco, alcohol, or firearms).

Applying for an EIN can be done online by visiting the EIN Assistant website, and following their application procedure. Remember to incorporate your business before you begin the application because you will be asked for your business's formation date and legal name (this is the name that appears on your business certificate).

Avoid putting this formality off for a later time because there are a few business opportunities that hinge on it, such as:

- **Most banks will expect you to have an EIN when applying for a business bank account.** Having a business bank account will be necessary when you start generating profits from your business, when you apply for a business credit card, or when seeking a business loan.
- **An EIN will also be necessary when you start looking into growing your team.** As a business owner, you will need an EIN to set up payroll, and the IRS will need the number to track payroll taxes.
- **If you are running a limited liability company, the EIN helps to separate you from your business.** All of the

profits and losses of the business are recorded under the EIN, instead of your personal SSN. This will protect you from being liable for your business debts.

Due to the nature of the vending machine business, you will be expected to pay sales and use tax. Sales tax is the tax paid to the state revenue services for the sale of certain goods. Use tax is similar to sales tax; however, instead of it being levied on goods sold, it is levied on products or services the business bought and used, without paying sales tax on the initial sale. Every state will have its own list of taxable vending machine goods, and those that are exempt from tax. For now, we will look at the guidelines set by the Minnesota Department of Revenue, so you can get an idea about the types of products that are taxable.

Prior to July 2017, all food and beverages sold through a vending machine were considered taxable by a supplier. However, new tax laws listed the following goods as taxable by a supplier:

- soft drinks
- candy
- hot coffee/cocoa
- sports drinks (and dietary supplements)

Goods that are exempt from tax include:

- bottled water
- licorice
- milk cartons
- muffins

There are also a few hygiene and grooming products sold through vending machines which are taxable by a supplier, such as:

- cosmetics
- condoms
- baby lotions
- shampoo
- deodorants
- soaps
- toothpastes / toothbrushes
- sunscreens / suntan lotions

Tax-exempt hygiene and grooming products include:

- diapers
- baby bottles
- pacifiers
- teething rings
- feminine hygiene products

Sales of other miscellaneous products sold through vending machines that are taxable include:

- reading books
- notebooks
- coloring pencils
- magazines
- newspapers
- souvenirs
- laundry detergents

- fabric softeners
- sewing kits
- phone cards

The following miscellaneous products sold through vending machines are tax exempt; these include:

- over-the-counter drugs
- clothing items
- clothing accessories
- cigarettes

Products or equipment that you use to run your vending machine business are taxable, unless stated otherwise. Once again, check with your state revenue services to see the guidelines of taxable and non-taxable goods. Below are examples of taxable purchases as dictated by the Minnesota Department of Revenue. If you have not paid sales tax on the following items, you will need to pay use tax:

- general business supplies (i.e. laptops, cell phones, office equipment and supplies, cleaning supplies, computer software, etc)
- utilities (i.e. water, electricity, internet, postage, gas, etc)
- taxable services (i.e. insurance, security, vending machine repair or maintenance, etc)
- purchase or new or used vending machines
- machine parts and repair labor

It's important to note that you are not required to pay sales tax to suppliers on goods intended for resale (goods that will be sold through your vending machine). This is because you are going to pay sales tax when you complete your own sales tax return during tax season. Instead, provide your supplier with a filled-out Form ST3 Certificate of Exemption, and specify that you are going to resell their goods. If you do end up paying sales tax on goods for resale, you can deduct the sales tax you paid on your sales tax return.

During tax season, you will need to calculate sales tax on both taxable and non-taxable goods sold through your vending machine. You can calculate sales tax on total taxable receipts. You are not allowed to deduct costs like machine rental, location rental, or cost of goods sold. If the owner of the location demands a fee or commission from every sale, you need to calculate sales tax before making these deductions.

OPENING A BANK ACCOUNT

The next legal hurdle you will need to cross is opening a business bank account. There are many reasons why this is beneficial for your business, especially if you have incorporated a limited liability business. Having a business bank account separates your finances and assets from your business finances and assets. It also helps you build healthy credit and makes filing taxes and accounting a lot easier!

A great option for building credit is to open a net 30 account. This is like a business line of credit where you can purchase goods now and pay the full balance within 30 days. Net 30 credit vendors are not necessarily banking institutions; however, they report all payments to commercial credit unions, which can boost your business's credit profile. Keep in mind that if you don't pay on time, it can negatively impact your business's credit profile.

If you are not able to get a net 30 account, you can apply for a business credit card. Your banking service provider will help you complete an application for a business credit card. If used responsibly, it can also help you build your business's credit profile and increase the number of financing options available to you.

The small business website TRUIC conducted research on the best national banking institutions in the U.S. for small businesses (TRUIC, 2022). These ranged from online banks to brick-and-mortar banks, and those that offered low to zero fees. Their criteria for selecting the best banks came down to these four factors:

- the type of business
- specific banking needs of the business
- bank requirements for opening an account
- other banking features

Five national banks were chosen as being the most accommodating to small businesses for the year 2022. These five banks were placed in five different categories, which were as follows:

1. Best Credit Union: Navy Federal Credit Union

Navy Federal offers small businesses a choice between three different checking accounts, two savings accounts, and business CDs. Their small business checking account comes with a 0.5%

interest rate, zero monthly service fees, and the first 30 non-electronic transactions free (thereafter charging $0.25 per transaction). The only downside is that you need to have a personal checking account opened with them before you can open your business account, and to do that you must be affiliated with someone who works or has retired from the military forces.

2. Best Online Bank: BlueVine

If you prefer to complete most of your banking needs online, and do few cash transactions per month, then you should consider opening an account with BlueVine. The bank started as a small business money lender and grew to offer banking solutions. Their online checking account has no monthly, non-sufficient funds, or income wire fees. It doesn't enforce a minimum bank balance, but rewards you with 1% interest on balances over $1,000. The only downside is that it doesn't have any physical branches, although it makes up for it with their online customer support.

3. Best Brick-and-Mortar Bank: Chase Bank

If you are planning on operating a cash vending machine, then you will need to collect money from your machine each week and deposit it into your bank account. In this case, you will need to open a business account with a brick-and-mortar bank where you can go to make large cash deposits. Chase Bank is a great option for businesses that make frequent cash deposits, and operate from multiple locations. There are more than 4,700 Chase branches across the U.S. and over 16,000 ATMs to choose from. There are a variety of business accounts available to business owners, and the fees on these accounts are relatively low.

Moreover, when you link multiple accounts together, Chase offers you higher interest rates.

4. Best Bank for Seeking SBA Loan: Wells Fargo

When seeking funding for your small business, it's important to consider a bank that offers perks, like small business lending. One of the largest banks in the U.S, Wells Fargo, specializes in small business lending, particularly approvals for Small Business Administration (SBA) loans. The bank also has a variety of business checking accounts to choose from, as well as merchant accounts and payroll services.

5. Best No-Fee Business Checking Account: US Bank

The best way to save money on monthly banking fees is to open a no-fee bank account. This type of business bank account may come in handy during the first months when there are few monthly transactions occurring. While many banks offer no-fee accounts, the U.S. Bank no fee business checking account comes with remote check deposits, mobile banking, merchant account services (so you can accept credit cards), overdraft protection, and check fraud prevention.

It is difficult to select the best bank for small businesses, since each of these banks offers tailored services that fulfill different business needs. When deciding on a bank to partner with, think about the features that would help you keep your business afloat during the early stages. You can always upgrade to a different type of business account, or different bank, later down the line.

OBTAINING LICENSES AND PERMITS

The type of licenses and permits you will need to operate a vending machine will vary depending on your state or county. Thus, you will need to check with your local authorities to find out what licenses and permits you need, and how much they cost. Licenses and permits may also depend on the kinds of products you are selling. For example, in some states you will need separate licenses for selling food and beverages.

Licenses and permits can be categorized into three levels of government: federal, state, and city/county. You may not need licenses and permits on all three levels, but it is worth checking with your local authorities to make sure your business is compliant. Here is a brief explanation of the type of licenses and permits you might need in each level of government:

1. Federal

According to the FDA, if you are selling certain foods and beverages, your business will need to comply with federal, state, and local regulations. If you have questions about the type of food products you can sell in your vending machine, speak to the FDA District Office and your local authorities. Moreover, in accordance with the Americans with Disability Act (ADA), you will need to make sure your vending machine is installed in a location that is easily accessible to people with mobility disabilities (read the ADA Small Business Primer to find out how).

2. State

You may also be required to apply for licenses and permits on a state level. Each state will have their own regulations regarding

WALTER GRANT & MATT COLEMAN

the type of products business owners can sell in their vending machines. Bear in mind that the location of your vending machine might also play a factor when it comes to the type of restrictions you will need to comply with. For example, vending machines installed in schools may be restricted from selling certain products, like tobacco or over-the-counter medication. Below are examples of state regulations pertaining to operating vending machines (Candy Machines, n.d.):

- **Florida:** Vending machine businesses must obtain a license before operations commence. Without a license, authorities may shut the operation down or issue a fine.
- **California:** Business owners must obtain a seller's permit to operate as many vending machines as they like. However, a seller's permit is not required when non-taxable products are sold in machines, or when products cost less than 15 cents.
- **Arizona:** After the Arizona government started cracking down on childhood obesity, regulations pertaining to vending machines became much stricter. Foods of minimal nutritional value (FMNV) are not allowed to be sold in vending machines, and there are tight restrictions on vending machines in schools, such as only 100% fruit juice and water can be sold and no vending machine sales can occur during meal times.
- **Colorado:** Vending machine businesses must obtain a sales tax license to run as many machines as they like, and every machine must have a decal.
- **Massachusetts:** Vending machine businesses must obtain a license from the commissioner. After the license has been approved, the commissioner will give the

business owner a label with their license number written. This label should be displayed on every machine, in every location.

3. City/County

In addition to obtaining federal and state licenses and permits, check with your city or county to find out if there are any more licenses and permits your business needs to legally operate. Examples of additional licenses and permits are vendor's license, resale license or permit, a local food service license, or a vending location license.

For more information on the required licenses and permits, it is advised to check with your local clerk's office or get assistance from one of the local associations mentioned in U.S. Small Business Association's directory of local business resources.

SIGNING CONTRACTS FOR YOUR VENDING MACHINE BUSINESS

It should be a requirement for your suppliers, lessors, and other business partners to sign agreements, or contracts, before working with you. These agreements ensure that whatever expectations were agreed upon are displayed in writing. Doing this will reduce the rise of legal disputes or misunderstandings between all parties.

Of course, each vending machine will enter into unique contracts; however, some of the standard contracts all vending machine operators are likely to enter into, include:

- **Rental agreement:** You might decide to lease your vending machine or rent out a location from a landlord.
- **Service agreement:** When partnering with suppliers, machine operators, and insurance companies, you will need to sign service agreements to clearly outline the terms and conditions of your relationships.
- **Certificate of occupancy:** Depending on where your machine is located, you may need to obtain a certificate of occupancy to confirm that all building codes and regulations were met by all parties.

Contracts are valuable because they protect your business from risky deals or fraudulent companies. For instance, one of the most important contracts you will sign is the one between your business and the landlord or property owner where your machine is installed. This contract will clearly stipulate how much you will pay to rent the space, or how much commission you will give to the landlord/property owner, based on gross sales. Some of the components to include in your contract are:

- vending machine model and type
- products sold
- rights to replace, increase, or decrease number of vending machines
- exclusivity clause (if necessary)
- duration of contract
- termination clauses

You can find free contract templates online; however, it is advised that you run your contracts through an attorney who can review and make necessary edits before any agreements are made.

Once you have secured all the necessary licenses and permits for your business, it's time to take a step further towards securing your business from both legal and illegal troubles by taking insurance coverage.

CHAPTER 11
TAKING COVER WITH INSURANCE

AN OVERVIEW OF BUSINESS INSURANCE

There is a constant danger of unforeseen death, disability, and destruction looming over businesses and the people who work in them. These risks may result in financial damage that sets the business back significantly. Taking insurance coverage helps transfer as much risk as possible to the insurance companies, in order to protect the business and its valuable resources.

Business insurance refers to a wide range of insurance services offered to businesses to protect them from financial losses. Even though business insurance is not mandatory, business owners, especially those running startups, take too much of a risk when they don't get coverage. For example, if your business received an unexpected lawsuit, or one of your vending machines were vandalized and needed immediate repairs, the absence of insurance coverage would mean that you had to pay for these expenses out of your own pocket.

Besides unforeseen lawsuits and vandalism, there are other reasons why you need to get business insurance, which are:

1. You are covered in the event of a natural disaster or property damage

Vending machines can be installed indoors or outdoors, but in all instances, they are placed under the auspices of a building. Business insurance can compensate you for the money you couldn't make while a building was being repaired from damages.

2. It gives you a crisis management plan for future uncertainties

Many businesses could not predict the Covid-19 pandemic. Those that had insurance coverage were able to claim for losses suffered as a result of business interruptions, and other losses in revenue. Since we live in an ever-changing world, which places a lot of pressure on domestic and foreign economies, it is useful for businesses to prepare for uncertainties.

3. You can save more money in the long run

Although business insurance is an added monthly expense, you can save thousands of dollars in the long run due to being protected against costly risks. It is better to pay a nominal fee every month than take out a loan or compromise the health of your business to pay for losses, lawsuits, injuries, or damages.

4. Some financial lenders may require you to have insurance coverage

Before lenders give you money to grow your business, they might want to see evidence of insurance coverage. Having insurance protects your business model and ensures you are using funds for the appropriate reasons—not putting out unexpected fires!

5. Having insurance can give you peace of mind

When a big company is hit with a loss, it may not set them back financially because they may have money in reserves. However, when a small business is hit with a loss, it can affect the stability of the business, and in some cases, lead to business rescue. Insurance coverage gives startup entrepreneurs peace of mind, knowing that they have a comfy safety net in the event of unforeseen losses.

INSURANCE FOR VENDING MACHINE BUSINESSES

There are unique risks that your vending machine business will be exposed to. Some of these risks include:

- the risk of theft or vandalism, especially when your machine is located in a public area
- machine malfunction that requires urgent repairs or maintenance
- credit card fraud
- injuries to customers caused by the quality of your vending machine products (i.e. a customer getting food poisoning after consuming one of your vending machine products)

There are a range of insurance products that can protect you against many of these risks; however, since insurance can be costly, you may not be able to cover every possible risk. Nonetheless, there are three policy types that are important for your business and can give you maximum coverage. These include the following:

Commercial General Liability Insurance: The most comprehensive type of business insurance is general liability insurance. For example, this can cover property damage, bodily injuries, medical payments, personal and advertising losses (i.e. making false claims in advertising), and legal defense and judgment.

Property Insurance: This type of insurance cover protects your business assets such as your inventory, owned or leased warehouse, or equipment (vending machines), from theft, losses, or damages. The price of your insurance premium will depend on the size or location of your property, model of your equipment, and value or quantity of stock. Some insurance providers will offer what is known as a Business Owner's Policy (BOP), which combines general liability insurance and property insurance under one policy.

Commercial Auto Insurance: If you have a vehicle that you use to pick up stock, refill your vending machine, and carry out other business tasks, you can cover the vehicle against car accidents, vehicle theft, and medical bills due to injuries incurred by the driver in transit. Even if you are using your personal car to carry out business errands, it is advised to take out commercial auto insurance since many personal auto insurance policies may not cover business-related accidents or expenses.

If you would like to extend your insurance coverage and include other types of insurance, here are a few that you can consider:

Worker's compensation policy: You can cover employees in the event of injuries incurred while working. The policy normally covers medical bills or compensates workers for the number of days missed from work.

Crime insurance: Since theft, fraud, and vandalism are real threats to your business, you can get cover to protect your business against losses due to crime.

Business interruption insurance: In the likelihood of your business needing to shut down, for reasons outside of your control, business interruption insurance will compensate you for revenue lost as a result of not operating.

Product liability insurance: In the likelihood of one of your compromised products causing physical harm to customers, product liability insurance will cover legal and medical bills in the event of a lawsuit.

THE COST AND CONSIDERATIONS FOR GETTING INSURANCE COVERAGE

An important factor when it comes to choosing insurance coverage is the price. Insurance providers set different policy rates, depending on the size of your business, location, type of equipment, and how much risk you are exposed to. However, if you are looking for average rates to help you set up a budget, here are some figures offered by the VendSoft company (Vend-Soft, n.d.):

- Your general liability insurance premium will depend on your sales turnover. For example, if you make

$100,000 or less a year, your premium can be between $400–$500 per month.

- If you are going to take out commercial auto insurance, your premium may be based on the model of your car and your type of driver's license. In general, premiums range between $750–$1,200 per month, per vehicle.
- The worker's compensation insurance premium can vary depending on the number of employees you have, as well as the benefits you seek to offer your employees. Your monthly premium can range between 3–5% of each employee's salary.

It is crucial to shop around and compare insurance policies and prices before settling for the best policies for your business. Remember, the best policy might not be the most affordable option, but rather the one that offers your business the most security. Before entering into an agreement with an insurance provider, read the fine print of the contract, including the clauses. If you cannot interpret some of the terms and conditions, hire an attorney to help you understand what you are getting yourself into.

Some of the expensive mistakes you should avoid when picking the right insurance policies are:

- not insuring all of the products you sell in your vending machine
- overlooking the need for regular repair and maintenance work on your vending machine
- going for the cheapest policy that doesn't give you comprehensive coverage

- overlooking the reality of crime, especially when you have installed your machine in an exposed place
- not insuring your vending machine, especially when they are old or leased

After enduring the tiresome process of complying with business legalities and insurance formalities, it is now time to talk about one of the crucial dimensions of any business—money.

CHAPTER 12
SCANNING THE COSTS

KEEPING YOUR COSTS LOW AND PROFITS HIGH

Your business has great potential to succeed due to the mass appeal of vending machines. In other words, you don't have to convince customers of the value of vending machines, since most who already support vending machines know what to expect. Instead, your focus will be on creating a buzz around your products so you can increase your turnover.

Profit margins will vary per product. In general, the cheaper it is to purchase the product, the higher your margin will be. For example, if you buy small candies for 5 cents each, you can sell them for 25 cents each and walk away with a 400% profit. Typically, snacks and beverages that can be bought in bulk can be sold for a profit of $1 each.

These profit margins may not get you excited, but the more you sell, the greater the amount of money you can go home with.

Besides selling out your stock, you can also make money by reducing as many costs as possible.

For example, the most expensive item you will probably buy for your business is the actual vending machine. However, you don't need to break the bank to purchase a machine. As discussed earlier, you have three options when it comes to the type of machine, but you can further reduce costs by opting for a refurbished machine rather than a brand new machine. Ultimately, this means that your machine can range from costing $150 to costing upwards of $5,000.

You can also find other creative ways of reducing the cost of your vending machine, like leasing rather than buying, or entering an agreement with a supplier to get a free machine. There are some suppliers that will lend you a machine with the expectation of buying all of your products from them only.

CALCULATING YOUR STARTUP EXPENSES

When thinking about the initial investment into your business, remember to do your own comprehensive research. It is possible to find a great deal on a machine on Facebook Marketplace, instead of buying one from a vending machine supplier. Doing your own research also allows you to compare prices and benefits, and choose options that are the most suitable for your business.

In this section, you will get a general idea of the kinds of startup costs you will need to factor in. There may be other expenses that are not included in the list that you will need to consider. Once again, it is up to you to do research and create a realistic startup budget so that you do not underestimate your initial expenses.

Below is a basic startup cost table that consists of common expenses for new vending machine businesses:

Refurbished snack and beverage machine:

$2,000–$3,000

Commissions paid to location:

5–20% of revenue

Storage space for stock:

$100 per month

Gas and transportation:

$50–$100 per month

Routine maintenance:

$50–$250 per year

Taxes:

10–37% of adjusted gross income

Transaction fees for card purchases:

5–6% of sale

General liability insurance:

$300–$1,000 per year

Vinyl or branding:

Up to $500

MASTER PLAN FOR COST CONTROL

Cost control is about monitoring your business spending so that you can minimize as many unnecessary costs as possible. In other words, it helps you to crack down on your budget and only spend on expenses that are essential to the running of your business.

Cost control isn't the same as cost management, although the two terms are often used interchangeably. Cost management involves creating a budget based on recurring monthly expenses. But cost control takes the process a step further by measuring actual expenses against budgeted or estimated expenses, and taking action when variances are found (i.e. when you end up spending more on an expense than what you estimated).

However, this isn't all. As part of your cost control system, you will need to find ways of making your monthly budget as lean as possible. This takes practice, and you will certainly get better at it with time. Reducing your expenses doesn't mean cutting out expenses, or going for the cheapest option all of the time. Instead, it is about creating realistic budgets, seeking the best deal whenever you are purchasing something, taking advantage of discounts or rewards programs, and keeping an eye on rising expenses.

Here are a few practical ways you can enforce better cost control in your business:

1. Understand your numbers

Remember the financial forecasts you drafted in the financial section of your business plan? These forecasts represent what you expected to spend when operating your business. Ideally your monthly fixed costs should not be more than what you originally forecasted, otherwise it will affect your overall profitability. Sometimes high costs are not due to your spending, but increases in product prices, transportation, or employee salaries. Look at your numbers constantly, so you can easily pick up on variances and rectify them quickly.

2. Take time preparing your budgets

A budget isn't merely a rough estimate. It is a cost management plan based on what you expect to spend or make during a certain period. To make your budget more realistic, use the latest market prices, and factor in costs like inflation, service fees, taxes, and so on. It is also important to get several quotes of goods and services before settling on an expense. You want to ensure that you are getting the best deals on products and services, so you can reduce as many costs as possible.

3. Monitor your inventory

You never want to put your business in a situation where you have run out of stock and cannot refill your vending machine. However, you also want to avoid having too much stock, which is stored in your warehouse and isn't being sold. Using product management software can help you track your inventory, and only purchase stock when you are running out.

4. Reduce the need for repairs

The only downside of purchasing an old vending machine is that it is likely to need a lot of repairs in the long run. Just imagine how expensive it would be to not only hire a repairman every so often, but to shut your vending machine down while it is being tinkered with. Before purchasing a machine, ensure it has gone through quality checks and has fully functional parts.

5. Use efficient time management strategies

The more intentional you are with your time, the higher your productivity will be—and the fewer frivolous expenses you will make. One of the best ways to save your time (and subsequently money) is to invest in automation, such as systems or software that takes care of administrative, marketing, or other book-keeping tasks for you. Another way to save time and money is to go paperless and save documents on digital clouds or drives, rather than file cabinets.

6. Minimize credit card debt

Maintaining a credit card can be costly due to the high interest rates and fees charged. You can reduce your spending in the short-term by making sure you use your credit card wisely. This will ensure you have a positive cash flow balance from month-to-month, and have enough cash in reserves to invest in your emergency fund.

You have attained crucial insight into the nitty-gritties of the expenses involved in a vending machine business. Now let's talk about how you can secure funds through reliable sources to meet your business's financial needs.

CHAPTER 13
RAISING CAPITAL FOR YOUR BUSINESS

FINANCING OPTIONS FOR VENDING MACHINE BUSINESSES

Every business requires funds to support financing the fixed machinery and regular operational costs. For a newly incorporated business, pumping the requisite funds out of personal savings can be challenging. This chapter will discuss the various financing options available to you to fund your business during the startup stages.

Compared to other startup businesses, the capital required to start a vending machine business is relatively low. However, not every entrepreneur has an extra few thousand dollars sitting in a savings account. For this reason, funding is necessary for most businesses.

The amount of capital your business needs will depend on the type of vending business you are starting (including the type of machine you wish to buy), the kinds of products you wish to sell, the lease agreement with your location site manager, and so forth. Therefore, before seeking funding, get your business model in order and know exactly how you plan on running your business—and how much it will cost you to run your business on a monthly basis.

Here are a few financing options you can consider when seeking funding:

Unsecured loan: This type of loan doesn't require the borrower to put up any assets as collateral. Lenders approve the loan based on the borrower's credit profile and history. Since unsecured loans present more risks to lenders, they tend to be strict on the criteria for approval, such as having a really high credit score. Examples of unsecured loans are personal loans and credit cards.

Short-term business loan: If borrowers have been in business for at least 12 months and have financial statements to prove it, they can apply for a short-term loan through their bank of choice. If approved, they will receive a deposit of cash into their business bank account and will repay the loan in installments, over a period of 18 months or less.

Secured loan: With this type of loan, the borrower puts up an asset like a car or property as collateral in the event of defaulting on the loan. This means that if the borrower is unable to pay back the loan, the lender can sell their asset to cover any financial losses. Since borrowers are putting up collateral, it is generally a lot easier for them to get approved for a secured loan than an unsecured loan. Secured loans also tend to charge lower interest rates, which makes them more affordable for borrowers with tight budgets.

Equipment financing: The most expensive cost when starting up a business is usually purchasing equipment and machinery. There are many lenders that are willing to cover the cost of equipment and machinery through equipment leasing or loans. The terms of these types of loans depend on the value of the equipment or machine. If the borrower defaults on the lease or loan, the equipment or machinery is recovered.

401(K) rollover: There are some vending machine suppliers who offer IRS-approved programs where business owners can access funds in their 401(K) without being penalized or being forced to pay income taxes.

Home equity line of credit (HELOC): Business owners who are also homeowners can take advantage of the equity accumulated on their home and take out a HELOC. Lenders will only charge interest on the amount of credit spent.

SBA loan: Loans that are backed by the SBA range from as little as $500 to as much as $5 million. They also cater to different business needs, such as purchasing equipment or providing working capital. Each SBA loan will have its own eligibility requirements; however, in general, these loans favor small businesses who have proven creditworthiness, and have a solid business plan.

The type of financing option you end up choosing will depend on your unique financial situation and the offers you qualify for. Shop around and speak to a financial expert who can help you make the best decision for your business.

113

LIST OF RECOMMENDED LENDERS

Take a moment and think about what you would do if your loan of $5,000 was approved by a lender.

You could buy 15–20 bulk vending machines, or 1–2 refurbished snack and beverage machines. The rest of the money would be spent on buying products for your vending machine and covering other monthly expenses like gas, insurance, and utilities.

Now that you have an idea of how much you need and where your startup capital would go, you can confidently compile a funding proposal, which will accompany your business plan, and approach the following list of lenders:

Fora Financial: Specializes in short-term loans for working capital, equipment purchases, and inventory purchases. Loans range between $5,000–$500,000, and your business is given 15 months to repay. Funding is made available as quickly as 24 hours.

Credibly: Specializes in lines of credit, short-term loans, SBA loans, and alternative financing. Loans for working capital are valued up to $400,000 and repayable within 18 months. Business expansion loans are valued up to $250,000 and repayable within 24 months. Funding is made available as quickly as 48 hours.

Fundera: Specializes in long-term loans, lines of credit, SBA loans, and short-term loans. Loans are normally used for working capital, equipment purchases, and real estate purchases. Businesses can get up to $600,000 funding, repayable over 1–5 years, equipment costs are repayable over 5–6 years, and lines of credit are repayable over 3–18 months.

Lendio: Specializes in long-term loans, short-term loans, lines of credit, and SBA loans. Funding is made available for business startup costs, purchases, and working capital. Businesses can get up to $500,000 for short-term loans and lines of credit, repayable over 1–3 years, and equipment loans valued up to $5 million and repayable over 1–5 years.

Crest Capital: Specializes in equipment loans of up to $1 million, and finances 100% of the costs. Businesses can get approval for most loans on the same day. However, only businesses that have been operating for at least two years (with proof of financial history) can apply.

National Funding: Specializes in equipment financing for up to $150,000. Businesses must have been in operation for at least 6 months and have a credit score of 575 or higher. Equipment purchased can be used or new, and there are no down payments required.

Currency: Specializes in business loans for business owners with bad credit. The company offers loans for all credit profiles and funding can be accessible within the same day of applying. Loans are valued up to $500,000 and repayable over 72 months.

HOW TO PREPARE A BUSINESS LOAN PROPOSAL

At this point, you have an idea of the kind of loan you are looking for, how much you would like to borrow, and which lending institutions to approach. Great! The next step is to prepare your loan proposal that will accompany your business plan.

Think of a loan proposal as your way of introducing your business and telling the lender why you deserve the loan, and how you will use it to grow your business. Unfortunately, lenders don't approve loans to every business that requests one, so you need to truly sell your business and leave very little room for doubt.

The core of your loan proposal will be the financial statements. Unlike the business plan, you don't need to add information about your brand, team, operations, or marketing. In essence, there are four things that lenders will be looking for from your proposal:

- loan amount required
- how the loan will be used
- how the business will repay the loan
- what the business will do if the loan cannot be repaid

Your business loan proposal won't be as long as your business plan. However, there are a few important sections that must be included, which are the following:

Executive summary: You can treat the executive summary like a loan request letter or proposal cover letter where you briefly state who you are, your business background, how much you need to borrow, and how the money will be spent.

Brief business overview: This section can be identical to the business overview section of your business plan. All you need to add in this section is your business name and mission, type of business structure, description of business model, current annual revenue (if any), and number of employees (if any).

Sales and revenue strategy: Even though you don't need to include a marketing section, you will need to have a section that describes your products, the cost and selling price, and how much revenue you plan on making every month based on product sales.

Loan request and use of the loan: Most lenders, especially SBA lenders, will want to know how much you want and how you came to this figure. Here, you will need to add quotes from suppliers, forecasted monthly budget, list of startup expenses, and so on. You will also need to include details of how you plan on using the loan.

Proof of repayment: In this section, you will need to state the ideal repayment terms for your business based on the loan amount you have asked for. Moreover, lenders will want to see evidence that you can meet monthly repayment schedules. Examples of statements that prove your ability to repay installments are your cash flow statement, profit and loss statement, and sales projections. If your business is currently paying off debt, you will need to prove that you can afford to take on more debt.

Personal and financial history of business owner: You will need to include a section with your personal financial statements, credit report, tax returns for the past 1–3 years, residential address, and copy of resume. You will also need to show how much of your own money you have invested into the business.

Copy of contractual agreements: If you have entered into agreements with suppliers or landlords, it is important to include copies of your agreements. These may include your lease agreement, franchise agreement, purchase agreement, or business partnership agreements. You can also include copies of business permits and licenses you have obtained.

There are many people out there who could provide you with the necessary capital for your business, but you'd obviously want to choose someone who is reliable and genuine. Be prepared for lenders to ask lots of questions about your personal and business financial information to evaluate your credit profile and risk. After securing funding, you can start thinking about long-term strategies for keeping your business sustainable, such as investing in automation.

CHAPTER 14
ENGAGING THE AUTOPILOT

THE VALUE IN AUTOMATING YOUR BUSINESS

As your vending machine business takes flight, there will be an influx of heavy numbers—both incomes and expenses. With such large data, it may become impossible (and also unnecessary) to take care of things manually. Fortunately, you can take shelter in technology to automate the painstaking processes of your business, and sit back and relax while you watch your numbers rise.

Automating certain processes of your business only becomes necessary when you are ready to scale your business. This stage usually comes after you have experienced initial growth and desire to make your business operate smoother so you can increase sales.

Scaling your business isn't the same as expanding your business operations. When you scale, you look at current systems, processes—and routes in the case of vending machine businesses—and think of ways of growing your business by making them function more efficiently. This doesn't require investing more capital, as would be necessary if you were planning on expanding your business operations.

Research from Deloitte shows that 73% of businesses are already using automation to streamline their operations, and many of these businesses are looking to increase their usage of automation software from 13% to 51% of their total operation processes (Horton et al., 2020). What does this mean? In a few years, the already fast-paced nature of most industries will move even faster, due to the scaling of operations and the demand for increased volumes and exceptionally high standards of service delivery and customer service.

FIVE STRATEGIC WAYS TO AUTOMATE YOUR BUSINESS

Business growth is something you are probably looking forward to. Nevertheless, it is important to have a plan put in place for when your current processes become too slow or unsuitable to cater to the increase in demand.

Here are five strategic ways to automate your business processes:

1. Identify Areas of Your Business That Can Operate More Efficiently

The first step is to think about areas of your business that are perhaps disorganized, moving too slow, or take a lot of your time. This might include stocktaking, managing communication with suppliers, creating monthly financial statements and reports, or marketing.

2. Create Standard Operating Procedures (SOPs)

Next, look at each of these areas and write down the steps involved in carrying out the procedures. Be as specific as possible when outlining the steps because this will help you later on when you are considering which elements to automate.

3. Identify Repetitive Tasks

Looking at the procedures to carry out each process, look for repetitive tasks that can be canceled out. Imagine that you were an employee whose role was to carry out the procedure, and find ways of making the process less cumbersome to perform.

4. Choose Procedures to Automate

Now that repetitive tasks have been ruled out, you have more straightforward processes to follow. However, your job is not done. Look at each procedure again and pick those that can be carried out by a machine or software, rather than a human being. In other words, look for tasks that don't require human effort and can be done by a computer without compromising your process.

5. Look for Affordable Software to Incorporate in Your Business

Contrary to what many business owners think, investing in automation software does not have to be expensive at all. Prices for software range from a few dollars per month to hundreds of dollars per month, depending on the features and use agreements. Before investing in any software, take advantage of free trials and request a demo so you can assess how easy it is to navigate, and whether the software offers the benefits you are looking for.

AUTOMATION-FRIENDLY BUSINESS TASKS

If you desire to structure your vending machine business as a form of passive income, then you will need to consider ways of automating the majority of tasks. While the use of technological tools and software can take over certain tasks, there will always be a need for employees to carry out specific functions of your business. Before we discuss the need for human labor, here are a few business tasks you can assign to a machine:

Emails, social media, and sales: There are apps and online tools that can manage your online reputation, track visitors on your website, and help you advertise directly to your audience on social media. These apps and tools have built-in algorithms that ensure the right people see your brand and support your business.

Accounting and billing: You can keep track of your finances by investing in a comprehensive financial management software that allows you to create custom invoices, keep track of receipts, calculate taxes, manage your monthly budget, and generate reports or forecasts at the end of each month.

File transfers: You can become a paperless business by creating, storing, and sharing files through digital channels. Some of the best platforms that support file transfers include Google Drive, Dropbox, and WeTransfer. You can also store important documents in access-controlled drives online, also known as the cloud.

Communication: Schedule and host your business meetings online, or create an online workspace on platforms like Slack or Asana where you can collaborate with suppliers and employees under one roof.

There are a number of apps and software programs designed specifically for vending machine businesses that can help you with the aforementioned automation-friendly tasks. Here is a list of some management software to consider:

Vend-Track: An online application that helps you manage various aspects of your business, especially when you are operating more than one vending machine in multiple locations. The application includes helpful features like Google Maps, printable location service sheets, and inventory reports. You can sign up for a 14-day free trial to explore all of the features the app has to offer, although bear in mind the demo has limited functionality.

Cantaloupe: This software comes with many different tools that help you scale your business, such as supporting card and mobile payments, optimizing multiple vending machines, and inventory and logistics management. The only downside is that since it includes so many tools, it can be difficult to navigate if you are not familiar with the program.

VMS: Vending Machine System is a cloud-based software that provides you with real-time tracking of the performance of your vending machine, and monitors stock so that you can be notified when certain products need to be refilled. However, similar to Cantaloupe, it can be difficult for beginners to navigate the software.

Quickbooks: This software is used by businesses in many industries. It provides a simple way to keep track of your revenue and expenses, and create custom invoices. You can use Quickbooks on a range of technological devices, such as your smartphone, computer, tablet, or laptop. It also comes with a downloadable mobile app that automatically stores your financial data in the cloud, and syncs the information across all devices.

As helpful as apps and software can be in streamlining your processes, there are some tasks that can be carried out more efficiently when performed by employees. Since having employees will affect your profit margins, you may be responsible for completing these tasks during the early stages of your business. Later down the line when your business has been growing and generating steady revenue, you may consider looking for employees to complete the following tasks:

Customer support: While it's possible to customize your vending machine so that customers can essentially work the machine on their own, there will be times when customers need to call your business support line about refunds, theft, or a faulty machine. They will want to speak to a customer representative agent who can offer them speedy service.

Repairs and maintenance: Even the most tech-savvy vending machines are built and serviced by qualified technicians. During the early stages of your business, you may decide to outsource a repairman, but later on when you operate multiple machines, you may decide to hire your own in-house repairman.

Quality assurance: Machines are not advanced enough to assess the quality of goods. You will need to hire an individual who can test products, identify defective items, and ensure that health and safety guidelines are being followed at all times.

Automation options are endless for your business. Plus, as you grow, you may need to switch from beginner-friendly and simple tools to more advanced and feature-rich tools—or move from part-time employees to full-time staff that work in shifts around the clock. When you finally reach the stage where you are ready to hire employees, conduct proper research on the subject of hiring. The more research you do, the better quality leads you will find, and the less time you will need to spend managing your business once they are hired.

If you have any questions about starting and running a vending machine that haven't been answered yet, the next chapter is dedicated to covering all the bases and making sure you are prepared for the journey ahead!

CHAPTER 15
VENDING MACHINE FAQS

FAQS ON OPERATING A VENDING MACHINE BUSINESS

We have strived to be as thorough as possible in explaining the ins and outs of operating a vending machine business. Still, there may be some common questions that have not been addressed thus far. Below is a rundown of some of the most frequently asked questions that have been presented with the aim to strike off even the last shred of doubt in your mind.

Question: How can a vending machine business offer exceptional customer service?

Answer: Since the vending machine business is mostly contactless, exceptional customer service is all about enhancing the experience of buying goods from your machine. Take time to consider the kinds of products that would delight your ideal customers, ensure that your machine is restocked regularly, and if you can, invest in a machine with built-in modern technology.

Question: How much time will I need to invest each month to run my vending machine business?

Answer: It isn't easy to give an exact figure; however, when calculating how many hours your business will need, think about the time it takes to collect products from suppliers, refill your machine, attend to faults and schedule repairs, and collect cash from your machine. If you want to reduce the amount of time you invest in the business, consider automating some key functional areas, such as inventory management and payment collection.

Question: I understand that vending machine businesses have low startup costs, but are they profitable?

Answer: The amount of revenue vending machines generate are based on a number of factors, such as location, target audience, novelty of products (as well as prices of products), brand awareness, and so on. Another factor that determines profitability is the type of vending machine and how expensive it is to maintain. Thus, one machine might bring in $5 per week, while another machine might bring in $300 per week.

Question: How can I minimize the cost of repairs and maintenance?

Answer: The best way to reduce repair and maintenance costs is to invest in a fully functional vending machine that can run around the clock with minimal service. When choosing a machine, go for a popular brand that has good customer support and produces reliable machines.

Question: How often do I need to replenish my vending machine?

Answer: You will need to closely monitor your sales volumes to determine the right time to refill your vending machine. In general, the more products you sell, the more frequently you will need to replenish your machine. Of course, not every product will need to be restocked—only products that sell.

Question: Are vending machines supposed to be washed?

Answer: Yes, it is important to regularly clean your vending machine, especially if you are selling food products. All you need is food-grade detergent, warm water and a clean sponge and towel. Since the inside of your vending machine is hardly opened, you don't need to clean the inside every week. However, the outside glass window and button area will need to be cleaned and sanitized regularly. You can also tie hand sanitizer to your machine so that customers can sanitize the button area and their hands while using your machine.

Question: How much commission should I be paying my site landlord?

Answer: It is up to you and your site landlord to decide how much commission to charge. However, bear in mind that commission is calculated on net sales and can reach up to 20% of net sales. Refer to the negotiation section of the book to read up about strategies to implement when negotiating commission.

Question: Who can I call to service my vending machine?

Answer: Vending machines have many different connected parts that make up the box that we see. It is therefore important to look for a trained vending technician who has experience repairing vending machines. The technician might come on site and diagnose the problem before drafting a quote. If replacement parts are needed, this will be a separate charge to the technician's call-out and repair fee.

Question: What is the best business structure to have for a vending machine business?

Answer: While all business structures have their perks, forming an LLC will offer you more tax benefits than other structures, protect you against business-related contracts and risks, and give your business credibility.

Question: Can I install my vending machine anywhere?

Answer: It is rare to find locations that are neither owned by individuals, companies, or the government. Therefore, before securing a location, you will need to inquire about who owns the space and contact that person, company, or local authority. Regardless of where you install your vending machine, however, you will be required to comply with local and state laws and regulations.

Question: How long does it take for vending machine suppliers to install a vending machine?

Answer: It typically takes vending machine suppliers 15–20 days to process an order and install a vending machine. If you are buying a custom vending machine, a representative from the company will need to meet with you to discuss your needs. Thereafter, you will need to give them time to customize your machine (the estimated time of completion depends on each provider).

Question: What type of electrical outlet do I need for a standard vending machine?

Answer: Standard vending machines run on 115 volts, at 10–12 amps. All you will need for a standard machine is access to a three-prong outlet. It's best to ensure this outlet is on a separate circuit. If not, ascertain from the landlord where to locate the circuit breaker in case the circuit is tripped by another electrical device.

Question: How much is a vending machine permit?

Answer: The price for permits and licenses vary from one state to another. However, the fee generally ranges from $10 to $250, depending on the license. In some states, business owners are required to complete a food preparation and handling course before they can obtain a license. Check with your state and local authorities for a list of mandatory permits and licenses.

Question: How can I brand and market my vending machine?

Answer: There are several ways of branding your machine. The most common way is to wrap your machine in vinyl, with your unique logo, colors, and symbols. You can also include signage, like having your slogan or brand story printed at the top or side of the machine. In terms of marketing your vending machine, you can create product promotions, special holiday-themed discounts, or start your own referral system.

No man is an island. Similarly, no business can run on its own. Your business will need help and support at different stages. Discover the various resources available to you that can support your business in the next chapter.

CHAPTER 16
SUPPORT AND RESOURCES

IMPORTANT RESOURCES

Some industries are swamped with industry support, resources, news, publications, and trade associations and organizations. And the vending machine business seems to be one among them. In such a dynamic market, it's imperative to stay abreast with top trends, technologies, and markets.

While you are still gathering information about the vending machine industry and other requirements to establish a vending machine business, be sure to visit the following websites:

- **Vending Market:** Website offering the latest news and trends about the vending machine market, technology, and equipment.
- **National Automatic Merchandising Association:** Founded in 1936, NAMA represents the U.S. convenience services industry. It seeks to provide

education, research, and support to its over 1,000 members.

- **VendSoft:** A vending machine route management software that can help you streamline your operations and manage your vending machines in real time. The VendSoft website also includes a blog and business guide, with many useful links that will help you get your business off the ground.
- **Vending Times:** An online publication releasing the latest news and trends on the vending machine industry.
- **Vending Connection:** Another great online publication offering vending trends and useful information.

If you are looking for support from other vending machine owners, you can join a few Facebook groups available online. Here are some popular groups to follow:

- **Vending Machine Tips and Discussion (26.8K members):** This private group provides a space for members to ask questions related to running a vending machine business.
- **Vending Machine — Buy, Sell, or Get Help (42.1K members):** This private group helps vending machine owners and restorers locate the right machines and ask questions about their machines.
- **Vending Marketplace (57.3K members):** This public group provides a space where vending machine owners or restorers can sell their machines, franchises, or vending machine businesses.
- **Used Machine Marketplace (51.9K members):** This

public group provides a space where individuals or businesses can sell machinery. Even though the products are not specific to vending machines, you may be able to find a seller who is selling their vending machine.

- **How to Start a Vending Machine Business (25.2K members):** This private group helps aspiring and new startup business owners through the early stages of setting up and running successful vending machine businesses.

Now that you have gathered all the information that you may need to start your own vending machine business, put it to good use and start working toward your dream today!

AFTERWORD

Getting a business off the ground takes a great deal of focus and passion. If you love the vending machine business model and can already envision how you want to leave a mark in the industry, you will undoubtedly have the focus and passion needed to survive the first few years.

The upside is that you don't need a lot of capital to get started. Depending on the type of vending business, machine, and products you sell, you may not even need to invest more than $1,000 initially. You have a lot of flexibility regarding how you want to structure and run your business, and which locations you would like your machines installed.

Let's face it—no other business gives you so many options on how to set up your operations, and on top of that, allows you to sell around the clock!

If you are hoping to add an additional income stream, start your passive side hustle, or leave your corporate day job, consider starting your vending machine business today, and don't live another day with regrets!

To review this book, you can:

- Scan the QR-code below with the camera on your phone to go directly to the review page.
- Or type in the Shorturl link below the QR-code in your internet browser.

shorturl.at/KQYRY

We appreciate your support!

REFERENCES

Allied Vending. (n.d.). *Vending machine license and permit guide - All 50 states [2021]*. Allied Vending. https://alliedvending.-com/pages/vending-machine-license

Beltis, A. J. (2021, September 2). *What is a business plan? Definition, tips, and templates*. Blog.hubspot.com.

https://blog.hubspot.com/marketing/what-is-business-plan

Bettavend. (n.d.). *From holy water to iPads: Vending's 2000 year timeline*. Bettavend. https://www.bettavend.co.uk/blog/history-of-vending#:~:text=America%20Keeps%20It%20Sweet

BizVibe. (2020, August 31). *Top 10 vending machine companies in the world 2020, top vending machine brands*. Bizvibe Blog.

https://blog.bizvibe.com/blog/top-vending-machine-companies

Bottom Line. (2012, April 7). *America's favorite chocolate brand? Snickers*. NBC News; NBC News.

REFERENCES

https://www.nbcnews.com/businessmain/americas-favorite-chocolate-brand-snickers-678964

Broaddus, H. (2014, November 4). *8 Important questions every business needs to ask their suppliers.* Www.linkedin.com.

https://www.linkedin.com/pulse/20141104143248-188260970-8-important-questions-every-business-needs-to-ask-their-suppliers/

Candy Machines. (n.d.). *Vending regulations by state: Vending permit requirements.* Www.candymachines.com. https://www.candymachines.com/Vending-Regulations-by-State.aspx

Catie. (2020a, August 7). *Best locations for vending machines.* 360Connect.

https://www.360connect.com/product-blog/best-locations-for-vending-machines/

Catie. (2020b, August 7). *Most popular snacks and drinks for vending machines.* 360Connect. https://www.360connect.com/product-blog/most-popular-snacks-and-drinks-for-vending-machines/

Chamber of Commerce of Metropolitan Montreal. (2009). *Negotiate the right deal with suppliers.* Infoentrepreneurs.org.

https://www.infoentrepreneurs.org/en/guides/negotiate-the-right-deal-with-suppliers/

Chen, J. (2021, February 22). *How an unsecured loan works.* Investopedia. https://www.investopedia.com/terms/u/unsecuredloan.asp#:~:text=An%20unsecured%20loan%20is%20a

Colestock, S. (2022, March 17). *The best equipment financing companies of 2022*. Investopedia. https://www.investopedia.-com/best-equipment-financing-companies-5083500

Conflitti, J. (2015, June 22). *25 Unique vending machines from around the world*. Healthy Vending Blog.

http://healthyvending.com/blog/unique-vending-machines/

Courier. (2021, February 9). *Inside the (surprisingly huge) vending machine economy*. Courier. https://mailchimp.com/courier/article/vending-machine-economy/

Crockett, Z. (2020, October 3). *The economics of vending machines*. The Hustle.

https://thehustle.co/the-economics-of-vending-machines/

Dinita, M. (2019, December 4). *Best 6 vending management software*. Windows Report. https://windowsreport.com/best-vending-management-software/

Eggspert, T. (2021, October 11). *8 Easy steps to start a vending machine business*. The Daily Egg.

https://www.crazyegg.com/blog/how-to-start-a-vending-machine-business/

Ennico, C. (2005, November 23). *10 Things to look out for when buying a business*. Entrepreneur. https://www.entrepreneur.-com/article/81176

Entrepreneur contributor. (2011). *How to find and work with suppliers*. Entrepreneur. https://www.entrepreneur.com/article/66028

Ferreira, C. (2018, December 16). *How to find a manufacturer or supplier for your product idea.* Shopify.

https://www.shopify.in/blog/13975985-how-to-find-a-manufacturer-or-supplier-for-your-product-idea

Forbes Agency Council. (2017, May 19). *Nine factors for finding the right name for your business.* Forbes.

https://www.forbes.com/sites/forbesagencycouncil/2017/05/19/nine-factors-for-finding-the-right-name-for-your-business/?sh=70420b7856ca

Friendship Vending. (n.d.). *What makes a good vending location.* Friendship Vending Company: Nashville's Vending Service.

https://www.friendshipvendingco.com/blog/what-makes-good-vending-location

Girsch-Bock, M. (2020, December 14). *5 Ways to effectively control costs in your small business.* The Blueprint. https://www.fool.com/the-blueprint/cost-control/

Gleeson, P. (2019, March 1). *Vending machine business pros and cons.* Chron.com. https://smallbusiness.chron.com/vending-machine-business-pros-cons-1363.html

Global Vending Group. (2014, June 12). *Should you buy a new or used vending machine?* Global Vending Group Inc.

https://www.globalvendinggroup.com/blog/should-you-buy-a-new-or-used-vending-machine/

Global Vending Group Inc. (2014, December 2). *4 Challenges to starting a vending machine business.* Global Vending Group Inc.

https://www.globalvendinggroup.com/blog/4-challenges-to-starting-a-vending-machine-business/

Go, G. (2020, February 3). *10 Ways to find a wholesale distributor.* The Balance Small Business. https://www.thebalancesmb.com/how-to-find-a-wholesale-distributor-2531713

Good Reads. (n.d.). *John F. Kennedy quote.* Www.goodreads.com.

https://www.goodreads.com/author/show/3047.John_F_Kennedy

Good Reads. (2019). *A quote by Benjamin Franklin.* Goodreads.com.

https://www.goodreads.com/quotes/460142-if-you-fail-to-plan-you-are-planning-to-fail

Griffin, D. (2010). *The effect of business location to the business' success.* Chron.com. https://smallbusiness.chron.com/effect-business-location-business-success-596.html

H, P. (2020, November 24). *How to start a profitable vending machine business?*

Quickbooks.intuit.com. https://quickbooks.intuit.com/global/resources/budget-and-planning/vending-machine-business/

Haut, A. (n.d.). *How to prepare a loan proposal.* Www.sba.gov.

https://www.sba.gov/offices/district/nd/fargo/resources/how-prepare-loan-proposal

Hayes, A. (2022, May 4). *Business plans: The ins and outs.* Investopedia.

REFERENCES

https://www.investopedia.com/terms/b/business-plan.asp#toc-understanding-business-plans

HealthyYouVending. (n.d.). *Healthy vending machine snacks from Healthy You Vending*. Www.healthyyouvending.com.

https://www.healthyyouvending.com/products/healthy-snacks/

Horton, R., Watson, J., & Schaefer, G. (2020, November 25). *Automation with intelligence*. Deloitte Insights.

https://www2.deloitte.com/us/en/insights/focus/technology-and-the-future-of-work/intelligent-automation-2020-survey-results.html

Huber, B. (2021, March 11). *Vending machine financing: Get a loan for inventory, and equipment*. Bestsmallbusinessloans.com.

https://bestsmallbusinessloans.com/industry/vending-machine-loans.html

IBISWorld. (2021, July 30). *Vending machine operators in the US - Market size 2005–2027*. Www.ibisworld.com.

https://www.ibisworld.com/industry-statistics/market-size/vending-machine-operators-united-states/

Indeed. (n.d.). *A guide to starting a vending machine business*. Www.indeed.com.   https://www.indeed.com/hire/c/info/vending-machine-business

Jaideep, S. (2015, April 11). *Product mix: Top 10 factors affecting product mix*. Your Article Library.

https://www.yourarticlelibrary.com/marketing/product/product-mix-top-10-factors-affecting-product-mix/48615

Josetti, A. (2016). *7 Reasons why insurance is important.* Hni.com.

https://www.hni.com/blog/bid/86285/7-reasons-why-insurance-is-important

K, S. (n.d.). *Simon Sinek - Dream big. Start small. But most of all, start.* Goalcast. https://www.goalcast.com/top-simon-sinek-quotes-hard-truths-success/simon-sinek-dream-big-start-small-but-most-of-all-start/

Kale, R., & Deshmukh, R. (2021, February). *Vending machine market size and share: Industry Research Report 2027.* Allied Market Research.

https://www.alliedmarketresearch.com/vending-machine-market-A09486

Knack, O. (2018, October 9). *Looking for suppliers? 10 Qualities of the best suppliers.* Intouch-Quality.com. https://www.intouch-quality.com/blog/5-qualities-of-a-good-supplier

Koman, T. (2019, May 8). *The best and worst pop-tart flavors of all time.* Delish. https://www.delish.com/food/g27396052/pop-tart-flavor-ranking/

Lindzon, J. (2019, May 1). *The importance of a business plan: 10 Reasons you need a road map for your business.* Wave Blog.

https://www.waveapps.com/blog/entrepreneurship/importance-of-a-business-plan

Longo, R. (2019, October 28). *Do you really need a business plan?* Duquesne Univ. SBDC. https://www.sbdc.duq.edu/Blog-Item-

REFERENCES

The-Importance-of-a-Business-Plan#:~:text=A%20business%20-plan%20is%20a

Minnesota Department of Revenue. (2019, September 30). *Vending machines and other coin-operated devices industry guide.* Www.revenue.state.mn.us.

https://www.revenue.state.mn.us/book/export/html/14241

Monsalve, E. C. (2020, November 4). *Why should you start a vending machine business? Cost, tips, advantages and disadvantages.* Www.linkedin.com. https://www.linkedin.com/pulse/why-should-you-start-vending-machine-business-cost-casta%C3%B1o-monsalve/

MyHealthNewsDaily. (2015, October 28). *Half of Americans drink soda every day.* Fox News; Fox News.

https://www.foxnews.com/health/half-of-americans-drink-soda-every-day

Paul, A. (2020, June 14). *Using automation to scale your team and service business.* Kustomer. https://www.kustomer.-com/blog/how-to-scale-your-business-with-automation/#:~:text=Automation%20makes%20scalabili-ty%20highly%20achievable

PaymentsJournal. (2019, July 10). *What percent of US vending machines accept cashless payments?* PaymentsJournal.

https://www.paymentsjournal.com/what-percent-of-us-vend-ing-machines-accept-cashless-payments/

PolicyBazaar. (2022, February 15). *Are you running a business? Here are 6 reasons why you need business insurance.* PolicyBazaar.

https://www.policybazaar.com/corporate-insurance/articles/6-reasons-why-you-need-business-insurance/

Porter, J. (2012, November 27). *10 Questions every entrepreneur needs to ask suppliers.* Entrepreneur. https://www.entrepreneur.com/article/224701

Ratcliffe, R. (2015, October 10). *Sugary snacks in hospital vending machines "send wrong message."* The Guardian.

https://www.theguardian.com/society/2015/oct/10/sugary-snacks-hospital-vending-macines

SBA. (2019). *Loans.* Loans. https://www.sba.gov/funding-programs/loans

Schwarz, L. (2020, November 18). *Save time and money: Automate your business.* Oracle NetSuite.

https://www.netsuite.com/portal/resource/articles/business-strategy/business-automation-examples.shtml?mc24943=v2

Scuderi, R. (2012, June 19). *10 Simple ways to cut business costs.* Business Trends and Insights; one-amex.

https://www.americanexpress.com/en-us/business/trends-and-insights/articles/10-simple-ways-to-cut-business-costs/

Smith-Petta, L. (2021, July 21). *How to start a vending machine business in 5 steps.* Fit Small Business; Fit Small Business.

https://fitsmallbusiness.com/find-vending-machines-for-sale/

Stowers, J. (2018). *How to choose the best legal structure for your business.* Business News Daily.

https://www.businessnewsdaily.com/8163-choose-legal-business-structure.html

Sweeney, L. (2021, July 9). *5 Advantages of running a vending machine franchise.* Www.pointfranchise.co.uk. https://www.pointfranchise.co.uk/articles/5-advantages-of-running-a-vending-machine-franchise-6787/

Team ZenBusiness. (2021, December 13). *7 Business tasks that can be automated to boost revenue.* ZenBusiness Inc.

https://www.zenbusiness.com/blog/7-business-tasks-that-can-be-automated-to-boost-revenue/

The Brand Boy. (2018, September 21). *Importance of good business name.* TheBrandBoy. https://thebrandboy.com/importance-of-good-business-name/

The Hustle. (2020, October 4). *We interviewed 20+ vending machine owners. Here's how much they make.* The Hustle.

https://thehustle.co/we-interviewed-20-vending-machine-owners-heres-how-much-they-make/

Thomas. (n.d.). *Top vending machine companies in the USA.* Www.thomasnet.com. https://www.thomasnet.com/articles/top-suppliers/vending-machine-companies/%22/

TRUIC. (n.d.-a). *Business insurance for vending machine businesses.*

Howtostartanllc.com. https://howtostartanllc.com/business-insurance/business-insurance-for-vending-machine-businesses

TRUIC. (n.d.-b). *What is an EIN?* Startupsavant.com.

https://howtostartanllc.com/what-is-an-ein

TRUIC. (2020, October 19). *How to start a vending machine business.*

HowToStartAnLLC.com. https://howtostartanllc.com/business-ideas/vending-machine

TRUIC. (2022, May 2). *Best banks for small business in 2022.* Howtostartanllc.com. https://howtostartanllc.com/reviews/best-banks-for-small-business

Vending. (2021, January 12). *How to get a vending license.* Vending.com.

https://www.vending.com/how-to-get-a-vending-license/

Vendpro. (2021, January 5). *When buying refurbished vending machines makes sense.* Vendpro. https://www.vendpro.com.au/when-buying-refurbished-vending-machines-makes-sense/

VendSmart. (n.d.). *Vending machine how to's.* Vendsmart.co.za.

http://vendsmart.co.za/Getting-Started.php

VendSoft. (n.d.-a). *Choose the best vending machine locations.* Www.vendsoft.com. https://www.vendsoft.com/best-vending-machine-locations/

VendSoft. (n.d.-b). *Guide to the successful purchase of an existing vending machine business.* Www.vendsoft.com.

https://www.vendsoft.com/buy-vending-machine-route/

VendSoft. (n.d.-c). *How to start a profitable vending machine business.*

REFERENCES

Www.vendsoft.com. https://www.vendsoft.com/vending-machine-business-guide/#insurance

VendSoft. (n.d.-d). *What type of vending machine business is right for you?*

Www.vendsoft.com. https://www.vendsoft.com/vending-machine-types/

VendTech Media. (2021, August 17). *The 10 best locations for vending machines.* Naturals2Go. https://www.naturals2go.com/best-vending-machine-locations/

Ward, A. (2020, November 19). *The appeal of vending machines in a post-Covid world.* Www.greaterbirminghamchambers.com. https://www.greaterbirminghamchambers.com/latest-news/blogs/2020/11/the-appeal-of-vending-machines-in-a-post-covid-world/

Wendor. (n.d.). *Vending machine supplier.* Vending Machines in India - Wendor.in.

https://wendor.in/wendor-all-features/

Wood, M. (2020, August 27). *How to write the perfect business loan proposal.* Fundera.com; Fundera.

https://www.fundera.com/business-loans/guides/business-loan-proposal

YEC. (2021, November 8). *Council post: Five strategic ways to automate business processes.* Forbes.

https://www.forbes.com/sites/theyec/2021/11/08/five-strategic-ways-to-automate-business-processes/?sh=43b5bfc22d80

CPSIA information can be obtained
at www.ICGtesting.com
Printed in the USA
BVHW070936160223
658644BV00006B/372